JAMES EDWARD TOBIN LIBRARY
MOLLOY COLLEGE
1000 HEMPSTEAD AVENUE
PO BOX 5002
ROCKVILLE CENTRE, NEW YORK 11571-5002

SHAWANGUNK

Adventure, Exploration, History and Epiphany
from a Mountain Wilderness

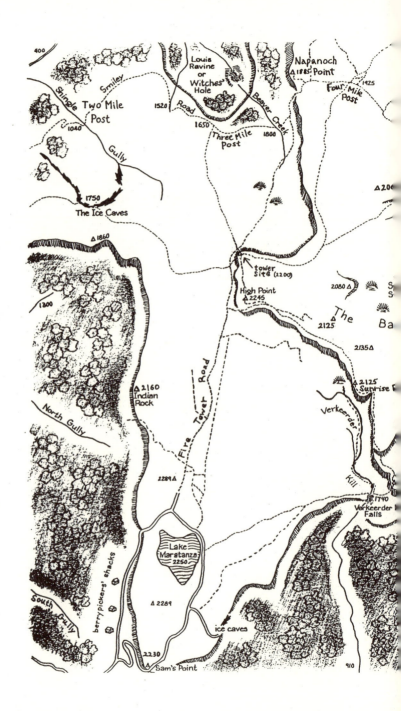

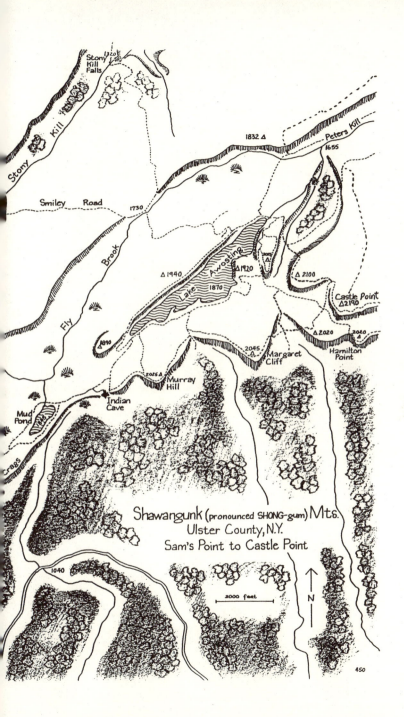

Shawangunk

Adventure, Exploration, History and Epiphany
from a Mountain Wilderness

by

Marc B. Fried

Copyright © 1998 by Marc B. Fried
All rights reserved.

Published by the author

    Please direct all inquiries to:

      766 Sand Hill Road
      Gardiner, N.Y. 12525

     Phone: (914) 895-3756

LIBRARY OF CONGRESS Catalog Card Number: 98-92466

ISBN 0-9663351-0-4

Manufactured in the U.S.A. on 60% recovered fiber (10% post-consumer).

Acknowledgments

I would like to express my appreciation to Captain Ray Wood of the New York State Department of Environmental Conservation (New Paltz office) for extraordinary help in making available documentary material in the office files, chiefly concerning Shawangunk forest fires. My thanks also go to Senior Forester Jack Sinsabaugh (retired), formerly of the DEC's Catskill office, for providing numerous copies of topographical maps that aided my study of the Shawangunk viewshed; to Paul C. Huth, Director of Research with the Mohonk Preserve, Inc., for illuminating many things for me over the years concerning natural history; to Kate Hubbs of The Nature Conservancy's Albany field office for additional sources on Shawangunk forest fires; and to Debbie Allen of Black Dome Press for advice and assistance in seeing me through the adventure of self-publishing.

Contents

Chapter *Page*

PART ONE

i	Panoramas and Perspectives	3
ii	Fire on the Mountain	24
iii	The Great Blaze of 1947	39
iv	Tales of the Long-Tail's Return	49
v	The Verkeerder Kill Revisited	62

PART TWO

vi	Interiors	79
vii	The Red Spruce Brook	96
viii	Flora	107
ix	Fauna	115
x	Atmosphere	134
xi	Exosphere	156

Part One

CHAPTER 1

Panoramas and Perspectives

THE SHAWANGUNK MOUNTAINS form the highest and most northerly section of a range that traverses portions of three states. In Pennsylvania it goes by the name of Blue Mountain. The Susquehanna flows through it, Interstate 81 passes over it, and the Turnpike tunnels underneath it. Farther east, highway 33 crosses the same ridge at Wind Gap, and at the Jersey border, where it takes the name of Kittatinny Mountain, the Delaware River carves a water gap out of it on its journey south to Philadelphia. After reaching a temporary apex at High Point, New Jersey at an elevation of 1803 feet, the same mountain drops in altitude and passes into New York. Here is where it takes the name Shawangunk, an Algonquian appellation whose pronunciation in the English tongue, established long ago from local usage, is *SHONG-gum*.

In New York State the range begins inauspiciously as a monocline of modest height and unremarkable form. At the Otisville Clove it dips to a low of nine hundred feet above sea level. From this point, however, the Shawangunks gradually but steadily regain stature on their way northward. The mountain passes into Ulster County, where state highway 52 crosses through a saddle in the ridge top, marking a boundary of sorts.

North and east of here the range undergoes a transformation: The sandstone cap rock becomes a pebbly quartz conglomerate of exceeding beauty and durability. The mountain gains dramatically in altitude and broadens considerably, its southeastern face crowned for miles by a great row of vertical white cliffs. Clothed in acid-loving shrubs of the heath family and severely stunted pitch pine, the rocky moorland of the mountain's plateau-like summit presents an aspect of wildness rarely seen below tree line in this part of the world.

From the abundant outcrops and exposed ledges atop the northern Shawangunks one may look out in clear weather upon expansive panoramas encompassing much of southeastern New York and northwestern New Jersey, portions of northeast Pennsylvania and northwest Connecticut, and points delineating the entire western border of Massachusetts. Learning to identify these places on the horizon was an early priority of mine after I'd become familiar with the rugged features of Shawangunk Mountain itself. But a time came when looking at these distant points no longer sufficed: If I could see all those places from the Shawangunks, it must follow that the Shawangunks themselves are visible from those many summits and ridge tops that constitute the Shawangunk viewshed. The visual perspective to be gained by traveling to the edge of the horizon and turning around to look back proved an irresistible idea, and I set out toward various destinations to see what I could see.

Before commencing my description of outings to these distant locations, I would be remiss to omit identifying a few of the local vantage points from which the Shawangunks may best be viewed. In the broad valleys of the Wallkill and Shawangunk Kill to the southeast of the range, a number of roads provide exceptional close-up views of the range, in favorable weather. Route 302 from Bullville north to Pine Bush parallels the Sullivan County Shawangunks but offers superb views northward to the highest part of the range as well. Continuing north toward New Paltz along the road that passes through the hamlets of Dwaarkill and Bruynswick, our attention is drawn to Sam's Point, Castle Point, and Gertrude's Nose in succession, and there's a dramatic glimpse into the sinuous ravine of the Palmagat. Beyond Bruynswick, as we head through farming country toward Benton's Corners, the breathtaking precipice of Millbrook Mountain dominates the scene, with the angular skyline of the Shawangunk escarpment stretching northward to its final dramatic surge at Sky Top, above Mohonk Lake.

Another lookout point from a lesser-known road provides perhaps the finest all-encompassing view of the southeast face of the range. This is obtained from the top of Sand Hill in the town of Shawangunk, where a road climbs from the Wallkill River crossing at Galeville and is met by another road coming south from Gardiner. From this point there unfolds an unobstructed panorama of the length of the Shawangunks from Otisville northeastward to Tillson, a distance of nearly thirty-four miles. Castle Point is front and center at a distance of seven miles. To the left of Sam's Point and right of Mohonk, the mountain declines in elevation as it moves farther away, creating an illusion that enhances the perception of vast distance.

On the northwest side, state highway 209 runs the length of the Shawangunk ridge. Between Napanoch and Ellenville are the best views, including a good look into Louis Ravine or the Witches' Hole, which carves up the mountainside behind the state reformatory. Because of the convex curve of the mountain slope on this side, the ridge top itself can best be viewed by climbing the elevations set back a ways from the foot of the mountain. There's a view from Cherrytown Road (off Pataukunk Road) in the town of Rochester, across an open meadow a little west of the Pine Grove ranch, and there are dramatic glimpses—though unfortunately no broad panoramas—approaching Napanoch, eastbound on Irish Cape Road and approaching Ellenville, eastbound on Briggs Highway and Route 52.

Looking southeast and south from the top of the Shawangunk Mountains, Mount Beacon, the Hudson Highlands, and Schunemunk Mountain form parts of the horizon. Their distances are moderate and their viewing angles nearly perpendicular to the axis of the Shawangunk range. The more interesting views originate from more distant points, farther to the southwest and northeast, whence come the lower angles that allow perspectives not readily obtained from sites nearby to the Shawangunks.

Looking south and southwestward, Schunemunk is superseded by another range called Bellvale Mountain. To this succeeds Wawayanda Mountain in New Jersey, on which are located the ski slopes of Vernon Valley/Great Gorge.

I made a summertime trip to these ski slopes, where I knew the absence of trees would permit an open view toward the Shawangunks. When I phoned ahead to see if the chair lifts were running and what the price of admission would be, I learned that in the warm season this development is transformed into an amusement park where "only" twenty-four bucks would entitle me to unlimited rides. But I asked for the manager, who was gracious enough to arrange for a free pass after I explained the purpose of my visit.

When I arrived, I rode the "Alpine Slide" chair lift as far as it went and then walked diagonally uphill and to the right along the ski slope, to where another chair lift passes overhead. From here I enjoyed a full view down the slope to the northern Shawangunks, all the way to Bontecou Crag, forty-seven miles distant. Leftward of Losee's Hill, Catskill summits protrude from behind the Shawangunks, but to the right, the latter form the final horizon. With binoculars, the bumpy outline of Murray Hill and the small gap in the ridge just south of Mud Pond are clearly visible; this gap is even barely discernible unaided. Especially dramatic are the drop-off in the ridge line to the right of the Millbrook cliff and the mountain's profile thence northeastward to Mohonk.

On the same day as my visit to the ski slopes on Wawayanda Mountain, I sought and found an equally good view of the Shawangunks from Route 17-A, east of Warwick, N.Y. Here there is no ticket to obtain, and the view isn't compromised by overhead lifts or noisy crowds. Four and one-quarter miles from the Route 94 junction, I turned left onto Kain Road at the top of the Bellvale ridge and immediately parked my car. It's a short walk back down Route 17-A to where a power line crosses, and at this point, to the right, there is easy access to the top of the Mount Peter ski slope.

The Shawangunks are visible without obstruction, from near the state line all the way to beyond Sky Top. The latter lies at a distance of thirty-six miles. Sam's Point, which has a bit of Peekamoose peeking up from behind, is twenty-nine miles distant. The view from this location is best enjoyed early in the day, with the morning sun illuminating the cliffs. The talus slopes beneath Millbrook Mountain are strikingly visible. There is a fine view of the cliff line forming the western edge of the Badlands and eastern wall of the upper Verkeerder Kill basin. With the aid of binoculars I easily identified the highest point in this cliff (Sunrise Rock), which juts out to form a partial profile against Cornell Mountain in the Catskills. (An even better profile may be obtained by following Kain Road down the mountain for one-third of a mile from the ridge-top intersection.)

With a short walk down the ski slope, the view opens up to the left as far as High Point, N.J. When I returned to the highway, I crossed to the other side and scrambled up a steep embankment to get a look from beneath the power line. From here more of the Kittatinny Mountains come into view, and there's an uninterrupted panorama of fifty miles of Kittatinny/

Shawangunk ridge line.

Looking from the Shawangunks (except from Sam's Point), most of the ridge rightward of Wawayanda is blocked by a nearer New Jersey elevation called Pochuck Mountain, which appears almost as a rightward continuation of Wawayanda, though actually it lies in front. There is then a clear line of demarcation between the right edge of Pochuck and the more distant ridge behind it. From Sam's Point, which is higher and a bit nearer to these New Jersey ranges and has a more favorable viewing angle, the distant skyline rightward from Wawayanda is visible over top of Pochuck.

On days when even a bit of haze is in the air, there appears to be a large, level gap as one looks farther to the right, until the Kittatinny Mountains begin, just to the left of High Point. On these days a part of the horizon often seems to be swallowed up inside this hole in a distant blue haze. (In the foreground in front of this gap is a series of high hills, visible from up close along Interstate 84 between Middletown and the crossing of the Shawangunk ridge.) In sharp, clear weather, however, especially when viewed from Sam's Point or Castle Point, the precise horizon can be accounted for across the entire breadth of this gap: The ridge extending rightward past Pochuck Mountain continues all the way to Allamuchy Mountain, where Interstate 80 crosses the range and intersects Route 517. These hills of only 1000 to 1250 feet above sea level are distinguishable at a distance of sixty to sixty-two miles from Castle Point. Farther to the right, some nearer hills form the horizon. These are eight hundred to nine hundred feet high and lie along Route 565, just east and south of Pelletown, N.J. To the right of these hills when seen from the Shawangunks, there is a more distant elevation, called Jenny Jump Mountain, that appears near the foot of the Kittatinnies. Jenny Jump is 1134 feet high and sixty-four miles from Castle Point. From the latter and from Sam's Point, its mammoth communications tower is sometimes visible with the aid of binoculars. I have visited Allamuchy and Jenny Jump mountains and found them to be heavily wooded and apparently lacking in vantage points that would permit views northeastward toward the Shawangunks.

From nearly every south- or east-facing overlook in the Ulster County Shawangunks, High Point, N.J. can be seen in favorable weather. Often its 220-foot summit monument is visible as well. The point is forty miles from the Mohonk tower and twenty-nine miles distant from Sam's Point. Except from the latter, it may not be obvious to the observer that High Point is located on the same ridge of which the Shawangunk Mountains are the northernmost segment.

High Point is accessible via an automobile road. I should say at the outset that climbing the stairs to the top of the monument itself is a waste of time, for this structure was apparently built to be seen from afar, and is useless as an observation tower: Its windows are small, rather filmy, recessed, and mesh-covered. But the view from the mountaintop at the base of the monument is magnificent, and the centerpiece of this panorama is the northern Shawangunk range, seen in cross section from this exceptional perspective. The Sam's Point massif predominates, but the eyes are soon drawn to the southeastern precipices of the ridge top, whose skyline is placed in bold relief by the very low viewing angle. Millbrook Mountain and Sky Top are clearly visible. With binoculars the reddish-hued cliff face of Verkeerder Kill Falls is identifiable, and I suspect the waterfall itself may be seen, sunlit, in times of flood.

From a three-dimensional relief map of this tri-state region, I once took note of a mountain called Camelback, rising just to the southwest of Interstate 80, twelve miles west of the Delaware Water Gap. Camelback is 2133 feet in elevation, and from the map there seemed to be an unobstructed

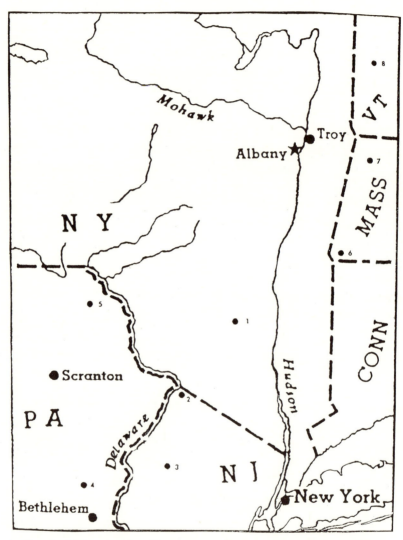

1. Castle Point in the Shawangunks; 2. New Jersey's High Point; 3. Hill near Allamuchy; 4. Blue Mountain; 5. Mt. Ararat; 6. Mt. Everett; 7. Mt. Greylock; 8. Mt. Equinox.

sixty-eight-mile shot thence to the northwest slope of the Ulster County Shawangunks. Nothing between rises higher than fifteen hundred feet above sea level. With the aid of a compass and binoculars, I subsequently went looking for Camelback from the Shawangunk Mountains' High Point (above Ellenville), on a day with unlimited visibility. I was unable to discover the object of my search, though various distant points in that direction undeniably identified the Poconos, across the Pennsylvania state line.

On my visit to High Point, N.J. on what was probably the clearest day of 1987, I made sure to have a look at Camelback. It rose some forty miles to the southwest. The line of sight thence to the slope of the Shawangunks above Ellenville clearly passed northwest of my location, across a corner of the Poconos far less lofty than either of the two extremities or than the summit on which I stood. I determined to include Camelback in the day's itinerary.

I'd observed from my highway map that the mountain has a road climbing nearly to the top. A short walk took me to the summit, where stands a ranger station. High Point, N.J. was visible, of course, as was Slide Mountain in the Catskills, some eighty-five miles away. But on their way northeastward through Orange and Sullivan counties, the Shawangunks disappeared behind that relatively lowly Pocono plateau. This confirmed the observation I'd made from the other end, but seemed to defy logic, until finally I realized where the problem lay: The most distant of views generally have lines of sight whose midpoints pass across valleys scarcely above sea level in elevation. The midpoint of the line from Camelback to the northern Shawangunks lies smack across that Pocono plateau, which thus accentuates the bulge of the earth. (Slide Mountain was visible only because of its far greater elevation.) It was thus I was reminded of something I'd learned quite early in life: The world is round.

From Castle Point it is possible to look over top of the southern Shawangunks, just to the right of New Jersey's Kittatinny range. On the horizon, far down along the axis of the Delaware River Valley, a thin, pale-blue line is visible with binoculars in clear weather. This represents the Blue Mountains of Pennsylvania, from the vicinity of the Water Gap southwestward to a point about seven miles beyond the Route 33 crossing near Wind Gap. (Farther to the right, the eastern slopes of the nearer Poconos intercede, forming a more distinct blue strip, clearly visible to the unaided eye.) This view thus encompasses portions of the same range during its passage through three states, each with its own name for the mountain. At the farthest visible point, the distance from Castle Point is about eighty-five miles. The same ridge may be seen without binoculars from Sam's Point, which is several miles closer.

High Point above Ellenville is the premier observation post on the northwest slope of the Shawangunk ridge. From here and from the top of the escarpment running due north from Sam's Point, there are views westward across Sullivan County into Pennsylvania. From High Point, looking six degrees north of due west, a 2667-foot mountain is visible at a distance of fifty-seven miles. This is Mount Ararat, which rises fifteen miles north-northeast of Carbondale, Pa., just east of the Wayne-Susquehanna county line. Points along the same distant ridge top (Moosic Mountains) are visible intermittently, to fifteen degrees, thirty minutes south of due west, distant from High Point sixty-two miles. I have not visited these Pennsylvania locations, in part because I suspect their views of the Shawangunks (even if trees do not intrude) are less than spectacular.

Looking farther to the right, the Catskill Mountains dominate the skyline from across the Rondout and Esopus valleys. A dozen or so major peaks are readily identifiable. The best views from the Catskills toward the Shawangunk range are from the 3085-foot summit of High Point (attainable via a footpath from Peekamoose Road on the northwest) and from 3145-foot Overlook Mountain, easily accessible from Woodstock via Meads Mountain Road.

From almost all the northeast-facing overlooks of the higher Shawangunks, the Berkshire Mountains of New England stand in relief against the sky at the point where New York, Connecticut, and Massachusetts come together. Highest and most prominent of this grouping is Mount Everett, Mass., 2602 feet above sea level. It appears as a rounded, haystack-like dome rising from behind a nearby front ridge. Mount Everett is situated such that a line drawn from Sam's Point to Sky Top would point toward it like an arrow. it stands fifty-five miles from the Shawangunks' High Point and forty-four from Mohonk.

An auto road climbs to within a short walk of Everett's treeless summit. The view of the Shawangunks from here is inspiring, the latter's intricate cross section rising like a work of sculpture from the flat-bottomed valleys at either side. On the left, overlooking the Wallkill Valley, the vertical cliff of the Gertrude's Nose ridge is discernible, and a second, higher cliff just to the right represents the Hamilton Point escarpment. The dome of the Minnewaska-Castle Point ridge is next, followed by the line of the Sam's Point plateau against the southwestern sky. The cliff at the foot of High Point drops off to the right, followed by the curve of the mountain downward toward Napanoch. With binoculars, the microwave tower at Lake Maratanza is visible, as is the monument at High Point, N.J. The white face of Millbrook Mountain and the dome of Sky Top may both be seen, though neither forms a silhouette against the sky.

To the right of Everett when viewed from the Shawangunks, and second highest in this cluster of summits, is 2453-foot Mount Frissell, whose very top lies in Massachusetts but whose 2380-foot contour, on the boundary with Connecticut, constitutes that state's highest elevation. This point is visible from the Shawangunks before Frissell's south slope is intercepted by Brace Mountain, which lies on the New York side of the border. Connecticut then comes back into view a little farther to the right in the form of 2316-foot Bear Mountain, the last major summit in this group before the skyline drops more sharply in elevation to the right. (In front of Bear Mountain and partially blocking it is 2211-foot Gridley Mountain, also in Connecticut.)

Of all the points of prominence readily identifiable from the Shawangunk Mountains, none appears so distant as a certain small, pale-blue form rising from the far northeast, visible from the Shawangunks on only the clearest of days. I have long known it to be Mount Greylock, 3491 feet above sea level, the highest peak in Massachusetts. It lies forty miles north of Mount Everett and eighty-nine miles from High Point. I have examined Mount Greylock at times of flawless visibility, during the afternoon and also in the pre-dawn hour, when it forms a sharp silhouette against a clear, red sky. Before sunrise I've twice been able to make out, with the aid of binoculars, the hundred-foot monument atop Greylock's summit.

There's a low skyline that appears to extend leftward from Greylock itself for a short distance before being eclipsed by a closer mountain range, as one looks yet a little farther to the left. This first ridge is not a north shoulder of Greylock, but rather a distinct ridge called Brodie Mountain, which rises in the vicinity of New Ashford, Mass., west of Route 7 and slightly less distant from the Shawangunks than Greylock is.

The second, nearer elevation that eclipses Brodie Mountain is the Taconic range, along the New York-Massachusetts border, beginning with a 2458-foot summit. The latter lies due east of a point that is about midway between the hamlets of

Stephentown and Cherry Plain, N.Y. This range attains an altitude of 2798 feet at Berlin (or Macomber) Mountain and continues north-northeastward to the tri-state region, whence it follows approximately along the New York-Vermont line northward. From map study I determined this ridge should be visible from the higher Shawangunks for a fraction of a mile into Vermont before being blocked by a somewhat lower but nearer ridge that lies west of New York Route 22.

I drove to the region with a friend, one crisp day in late summer; we stopped at an overlook along the Taconic Parkway near Philmont for a fifty-five mile-distant preview of our hoped-for rendezvous with the Shawangunk Mountains from inside Vermont. Arriving near our destination, I left my car in a parking area along New York Route 2 where the latter passes through a gap at the crest of the Taconics. A footpath heads northward nearly along the ridge top. The tri-state boundary itself lies some distance down the east slope of the mountain; the Vermont-New York line then juts westward for about half a mile before turning north.

From a swampy saddle in the ridge top the path begins a moderately steep 170-foot ascent, entering Vermont less than a hundred yards east of the very southwest corner of the state. At the top of this incline is a nearly flat area with a maximum elevation of 2480 feet above sea level. The path bears slightly left, drops a little in altitude, then ascends again through a clear area, just as it begins to pass back into New York through Vermont's western border. From here my companion and I obtained our first open view in the direction we sought.

The Catskills were there, to be sure, with Overlook Mountain immediately identifiable. The mountain range west of Route 22 formed a near horizon about ten miles to our southwest. The Shawangunks were nowhere to be seen. I took out my binoculars and began to scan this southwest horizon. As my eyes became accustomed to the glasses, gradually I became aware of the merest sliver of an almost unimaginably remote ridge top, floating atop the nearer horizon like a mirage. This nearly transparent wisp of the Shawangunks' very crest had materialized out of thin air, exactly where I'd predicted! It had kept the date we'd made months earlier, when I had foretold the Vermont connection on the strength of cartographic calculations.

The Taconic ridge top crosses into New York as it proceeds north-northwestward. My companion and I followed the path a little farther, through additional clearings, to an elevation of 2530 feet near the summit of White Rock. Beyond this the range drops in altitude and the intervening ridge swallows up the line of sight to the Shawangunks. As we continued northward past that first clearing, an unexpected bonus awaited us: Sky Top became visible through a shallow notch farther to the left along the intervening ridge. It was vaguely discernible to the naked eye, and with binoculars the familiar skyline from Mountain Rest to Eagle Cliff could be seen.

My companion and I had seen the Shawangunk crest as far rightward as Castle Point, over eighty-eight miles away. But the azimuth between White Rock (and its Vermont shoulder) and High Point passes a trifle too far north on the ascending, intervening ridge to permit a clear line of sight. This ridge that eclipses the Taconics when viewed from the Shawangunks does so beginning at a point about two miles northwest of Cherry Plain, eighty-two miles from High Point. Visible only during fine, clear weather, it soon appears to melt into a low, rather featureless horizon that arcs northwest and westward through Rensselaer County, remaining at a nearly constant distance from the observer atop the Shawangunk ridge.

Even at such a distance, not all of this horizon forms a final silhouette or skyline. For on the most spectacular of days, perhaps no more than once in a year or in a few years, a number of pale-blue summits may be seen jutting out unmistakably against the sky as one looks leftward along this plateau. These may be visible to the naked eye, but are more easily found with the aid of binoculars. The most northerly summit is only six or seven degrees to the right of the top of Overlook Mountain, when viewed from High Point. When conditions permit, it may be located by first finding a certain small but prominent formation, to the right of Overlook, that rises abruptly eastward from the Hudson Valley: This is a 1400-foot elevation lying south of Route 2 near Cropseyville, N.Y., about seven miles east-northeast of Troy and eighty-three miles from High Point. A little to the right of this formation is the northernmost of the summits.

A friend and I first spied these distant peaks on September 8, 1990, a day so fine that I was almost startled by the clarity of Mount Greylock and other familiar landmarks that normally appear somewhat hazy in even the best of weather. I was confused as to what it was we were seeing; only after subsequent map study did it finally dawn on me that we'd been treated to a rare phenomenon I had previously considered beyond the pale of credibility: a view from the Shawangunks deep into the mountain ranges of southwestern Vermont.

From the tri-state region, the Taconic range declines in prominence as it approaches the Hoosic River. The Taconics regain altitude farther north and east, on the Vermont side of the border, paralleling the Green Mountains, which lie a little farther east. Visible from the Shawangunks are several summits in Vermont's Green and Taconic ranges. The line of sight from High Point to the northernmost visible Vermont summit leads to Mount Equinox, 3835 feet high, near Manchester. The observer atop High Point who is fortunate enough to get a glimpse of this peak is looking across portions of six counties to a place on the horizon that is 119 miles distant.

For positive confirmation, I determined to make a trip to Equinox, whose summit is accessible from May through October via an automobile toll road. The opportunity presented itself almost exactly a year subsequent to my first sighting of Vermont from the Shawangunks, and my companion for the day was the same friend who'd been with me on the former occasion.

Visibility was superb, though a shade less spectacular than on our outing of a year earlier. From the top of Mount Equinox, a pair of mammiform domes (Spruce Peak and Grass Mountain) present themselves ten miles to the southwest. Over top of these twins, at a distance of about thirty-five miles, stretches the nearly level skyline of the plateau that curves between Cherry Plain and Cropseyville in Rensselaer County. near the right end of this plateau, just over top of the right dome, we could see Overlook Mountain off in the distance. With binoculars the Shawangunk ridge was faint but unmistakable, being most distinct at a point on the horizon that lies about one-quarter way rightward from the azimuth of the Spruce/Grass cleavage toward the azimuth of the southeastern foot of Overlook. All but the top several hundred feet or so lay hidden behind the intervening plateau and the curve of the earth.

Sighting Vermont from the Shawangunks begs the question of whether all six states in our viewshed might be visible from any one vantage point. Sam's Point sees only three states; High Point sees five, lacking a view of New Jersey; Sky Top's panorama excludes Pennsylvania, and Vermont is doubtful.

In search of a six-state view, I visited the highest elevation on the gradual rise two-tenths of a mile southwest of the south tip of Lake Maratanza: Here I was pleasantly surprised to find a sturdy, man-made platform of stones, four feet high, that affords a view over the tops of the scrub pine trees to Pennsylvania, New Jersey, Connecticut, and Massachusetts, in addition to ample views of the "home" state. But the Green Mountain State remains a question. The line of sight from this station would pass over, and to the left of, the point where the roadway first encounters the lake, at its northeast cove. Whether some of the Vermont summits might be visible over the treetops in that direction can only be determined on a day clear enough to actually see them if they're there. At any rate, the quality of the view from this location is diminished by the flatness of the nearby surrounding terrain on all sides.

Castle Point enjoys spectacular views to the west, south, and east, but the summit is just level enough to prevent a glimpse into Massachusetts and Vermont. If a low, rustic observation platform, perhaps fifteen to twenty feet in height, were ever to be built atop the summit rocks, it would reach above the treetops and afford a six-state panorama without equal elsewhere in the Shawangunk range. With a turn of the head, an observer could then view both Blue Mountain, Pa. and Equinox Mountain, Vt., elevations occupying Castle Point's farthest visible horizons. These lie within a fraction of being two hundred miles from one another—a distance encompassing eight-tenths of one percent of the circumference of the Earth.

Mount Greylock, Mass. lacks by thirty miles being the farthest point visible from the Shawangunk range. But it is this solitary mountain that rises most boldly and unmistakably from the distant northeast horizon, and it is visible from the Shawangunks on at least a few days during the average month. Long before I'd ever seen the more remote points in Vermont described above, the Massachusetts peak had become the object of my fascination: A view of the Shawangunks from that faraway summit had become the ultimate prize among distant points in the Shawangunk viewshed.

My first attempt occurred sometime back about 1980. I set out on an afternoon of superb visibility, with the idea of spending the evening with a friend in West Stockbridge, Mass. and driving up before dawn on the auto road that leads to Greylock's summit. My delay proved ill-advised: By morning a very slight haze had crept in, enough to obscure the farthest horizons. I could make out the Catskills' Overlook Mountain, at a distance of over sixty-one miles, but a view of the Shawangunks was not to be had that day.

I decided to try next time for a same-day, afternoon visit, with a sleep-over in the area on the night following. But my West Stockbridge friend moved somewhere else, and I preferred to avoid making the long drive there and back home in a single day. I could see no urgency: Visiting Greylock was something I would do someday when the circumstances were right, something I'd look forward to.

In 1988 I became friends with a young man from Great Barrington, and the idea of another attempt immediately presented itself. The autumn day I chose was one of impeccable visibility but gradually decreasing sunshine, as atmospheric instability began to generate cloudiness following passage of a cold front. I set out early enough to include Mount Everett in my itinerary and was successful in achieving my first view thence toward the Shawangunks. But as I looked northward from Everett toward Mount Greylock, I could see the possibility of the latter being shrouded in clouds—though the higher Catskills were cloud-free.

I stopped to pick up my friend, and we continued northward and upward, only to find the top few hundred feet of the mountain socked in. We passed a half hour warming ourselves at Bascom Lodge, the Appalachian Mountain Club accommodation immediately below the summit. A sign announcing "Notable Wildlife Sightings, Mount Greylock 1988" drew my attention to a journal in which visitors are encouraged to note their animal encounters. Among various reports of black bear, wild turkeys, etc., was this stirring account dated October 1:

"3:45 P.M. Chipmunk seen while picnicking on the summit."

The next morning I drove the nearly forty miles from Great Barrington back to Greylock for another try, arriving before dawn. The sky was clear and visibility excellent, but mist already rising from along the Hudson obscured the southwest horizon. What I did see in that direction was something that appeared as a small, double-topped mountain with summits of unequal height, reaching just above the sea of mist, a few degrees to the left of Overlook. Was this the Shawangunks? It did not look right, but I could not imagine what else I was seeing. The experience was obviously inconclusive, and I determined I must return someday for yet another try. Something rather unsettling dawned on me that morning: The view in the direction of the Shawangunks involves looking over the rooftop of Bascom Lodge—but from behind the lodge (and, ironically, only from that direction), treetops rose high enough to potentially obscure the horizon, even assuming perfect atmospheric conditions. Was my quest doomed? It was a question I could not yet answer. I amused myself by speculating on the utter futility of soliciting the park authorities of the Commonwealth of Massachusetts to remove the trees so as to complete Greylock's 360-degree panorama.

On my drive home, crossing westbound over the arched span of the Kingston-Rhinecliff Bridge, I was startled by a view of the Catskills' High Point, some nineteen miles in front of me. For I immediately recognized it as the mountain I'd seen in miniature, above the mist, earlier that same morning. I'd calculated erroneously that High Point would line up so close to Overlook Mountain as to be partially obscured behind it. I felt I had learned something of value and that I was now in a better position to locate and identify the Shawangunks from Greylock, next time around.

Next time came next year, once again in early autumn. The same friend accompanied me as I drove up Greylock for my fourth attempt. No sooner were we out of the car than I was astounded to see a clear, blue ridge top that was undeniably the Shawangunk range, rising from over the roof of Bascom Lodge: The offending trees had been cut!—apparently to open up the view from the sun porch of the lodge, which looks out in that same direction.

The sight of the Shawangunks from that vast distance is nothing less than incredible, and the ridge top from Mohonk to Ellenville forms the final horizon, silhouetted against the sky. With the naked eye I could distinguish the abrupt knob of Sky Top, seventy-nine miles distant; a dome representing the cross section of the ridge at Castle Point; and the Badlands/Sam's Point plateau. Between the latter and Castle Point a slight depression is clearly visible, marking the cleavage in the skyline along the axis of the Fly Brook. With binoculars, I could further identify Eagle Cliff, to the right of Sky Top; a portion of the vertical profile of Millbrook Mountain, similar to the perspective visible above treetops from the Clove, northeast of Mohonk; a profile of the cliffs northwest of Castle Point, descending toward Lake Awosting; and the drop-off to the right of High Point, similar to that seen with the unaided eye from Mount Everett.

Bontecou Crag lines up directly in front of (and lower than) Sky Top and is therefore indistinguishable. The cliffs of the Trapps are hidden behind Eagle Cliff. Hussey Hill, just south of Kingston, is visible to the left of Mohonk, and the Hudson River (a section of its width) between Hudson and Catskill may be seen as a band of reflective light at the foot of Overlook Mountain.

The Shawangunks occupy four degrees of the horizon, set off on the right by a lowland of approximately equal width before the Catskills begin. The right-hand part of the Shawangunk range, and the lowland itself, are both clarified by a very low, nearly flat-topped ridge representing the foothills south and southeast of Ashokan Reservoir. From the lofty vantage point of Greylock, one looks over the top of this ridge, which lines up with the bottom of the Shawangunks, practically with the floor of the Rondout Valley. The ridge in the foreground thus forms a horizontal line that helps to define the vertical dimension of the Shawangunk range. Virtually the full height of the Shawangunks is therefore distinguishable, especially along the profile of the mountain as it climbs up from Ellenville toward its summit at High Point.

It is difficult to describe my larger thoughts as I looked out across the miles to that familiar and beloved place, seen now from such an unfamiliar distance. But I think I understood something of what those first lunar voyagers felt, looking back at Earth. I was impressed by the stature of the Shawangunks, by the breadth and height and detail discernible even from so far away. One of the greatest satisfactions in life is to experience a long-sought and long-awaited event and have the living of it turn out to be even better than the dream of it had imagined possible: The sight of the Shawangunk Mountains from Greylock is something that all who love the Shawangunks ought to experience, even if it is only for one hour in a lifetime.

CHAPTER 2

Fire on the Mountain

> *But how the fires started up there don't ask me, I don't know nothin' about that; 'cause all of a sudden the whole mountain was afire, so whoever started it made a good job!*
> —berrypicker Bertha Van Leuven

LIKE THE HUCKLEBERRY INDUSTRY that spawned them, periodic wildfires raging across the crown of the northern Shawangunks are now a thing of the past. But until the middle of the present century, fire played an important role in the mountain's ecology and in the folk traditions of the people who summered at the huckleberry camps. By effectively pruning the berry bushes and burning off some of the competing vegetation, fires improved the crop and, incidentally, encouraged the predominance of pitch pine, whose resistant bark and heat-triggered seeding mechanism impart to it the status of a "fire-climax" tree. Even when an unusually intense blaze burned the pine trees themselves, their roots, usually undamaged, sprouted anew, giving birth to extensive areas of uniformly dwarfed forest.

Significant attempts at fire suppression by the State began in the early part of the twentieth century. Since the 1960s, the demise of the huckleberry industry has coincided with complete and effective fire suppression. Today a mix of hardwoods, including, increasingly, the homely and ubiquitous red maple, invades the mountaintop and the northwest slope.

Unless fire is reintroduced to the ecosystem, these hardwoods threaten eventually to confine pure stands of the dwarf pine to only the rockiest, most exposed terrain, beyond reach of its competitors.

A fascinating study by Charles Laing of the University of Massachusetts (Amherst) covers nine thousand years of vegetative and fire history and prehistory in the heart of the Shawangunk Badlands. Laing examined a sixty-two centimeter core of sediment extracted from the top of the Red Spruce Swamp, identifying pollen from various species and analyzing charcoal-to-pollen ratios. (The report was sponsored by The Nature Conservancy's Eastern New York regional office and presented in 1994.) He found that at the bottom of the sample, around 7000 B.C.,

> *pine dominated forests probably covered much of the Shawangunks as they did throughout most of New England. Oak and birch were also important and pitch pine was more prevalent in the Shawangunks than the surrounding lowlands. Jack pine may also have been present on the more exposed sites on the Shawangunk ridge. Fire may well have been an important component of this early pine forest before the immigration of many of the elements of the mixed deciduous forest. As pines decrease in importance grey birch increases dramatically but the absence of any clear evidence of fire activity suggests that this 'pioneer' species may [have expanded] as a result of successionary changes or disturbances other than fire.*

The early pine forest gave way to the birch dominance described above and, eventually, to a richer mix of vegetation: For a long period beginning about 4000 B.C., the Sam's Point plateau and Badlands may have held deeper organic soils sustaining a more diverse and taller-growing pine barrens community than what we see today. The relative absence of fire during much of this time would have permitted the accumulation of organic material to a greater depth.

Then, during the first millennium B.C., there began an increase of fire, with a dramatic increase about 400 A.D. Around the start of the second millennium A.D., a very high level of fire began which has continued until recent decades. Pitch pine dominance corresponds significantly, though not precisely, with this fire presence.

The cause of the establishment of this fire-dependent pitch pine community, the direct ancestor of the dwarf pine forest of today, is somewhat conjectural: Climate change resulting in more frequent or severe drought (and therefore fire) might have initiated the change. Once established, the dwarf pine forest would have been somewhat self-sustaining, because this kind of vegetation provides a highly flammable fuel. Furthermore, the presence of blueberry bushes that accompany this plant community would soon have been discovered by the Indians, as would the fact that the berry bushes produce best in burnt-over areas. It is considered quite likely therefore that the Indians may have begun burning over the mountain, at a point in time corresponding to the dramatic increase in fire in the early to mid portion of the first millennium A.D.

It would appear from the Red Spruce Swamp study that the dwarf pitch pine forest may have been most extensive from about 700 A.D. to 1600 A.D., after which the dominant position of pine declined briefly to a stable plateau, even as gray birch simultaneously increased. Throughout the course of the 1800s, fires from hemlock and woodcutting debris related to the tanning, hoop-making, and charcoal industries probably generated the highest temperatures in local fire history. While this may have been a factor favoring gray birch over pitch pine, the change clearly antedates this period.

When the huckleberry pickers of the nineteenth and twentieth centuries set fire to the mountain, ecological aesthetics were hardly their motive. They were interested in maintaining a vigorous berry crop and, in some instances, in gaining temporary employment as fire fighters. Doubtless there were also a few among them who simply enjoyed the sight of a good blaze. Although a burning that occurred during the berry season may often have been viewed as something of a necessary nuisance by the pickers, many of the largest fires of this century occurred in spring or fall. The blaze of July 1939 coincided with the picking season, but it was apparently a poor summer for berries, due to prolonged drought as well as to the lack of recent fire. Many of the pickers may have felt that under these circumstances, fighting fire was at least as profitable as picking huckleberries.

The earliest reference I know of to berrypickers' fires in the Shawangunks appears in *The Ellenville Journal* for May 4, 1872. The article describes a spectacular mountain fire visible from the village, on the west slope of the ridge, south of Ellenville and opposite to Leurenkill, "from the line of the railroad to the top of the mountain. . . ." The area burned was probably the rocky slopes northwest of Cragsmoor. This section would have been more clearly visible from Ellenville (and more flammable) than the recesses of South Gully, which lies more directly across from Leurenkill. The article states, "It is generally supposed that these fires were caused by sparks from the . . . locomotive—though it is the season when parties in the huckleberry interest are accustomed to start mountain-fire."

The *Second Annual Report* of the New York State Forest Commission, 1886 speaks more explicitly about the role of the berrypickers:

Berry pickers are here credited with starting many of

27

Huckleberry Pickers at Sam's Point

the fires. The proximity of the New York market and the great demand for the really fine quality of the whortle-berries, which abound on the mountain sides, . . . has caused this class of people to adopt the custom of burning over the fields, with a view of increasing the yield. This is done every year or so. . . . The Ellenville Water Works Company suffers from this cause, and a vigorous effort is being made to protect the part of the Shawangunk mountains occupied by the watershed from which they gather their water supply. It is said that the whortle-berry crop on these mountains, in the neighborhood of Ellenville, is worth from four to five thousand dollars annually, and also that there are houses and lots in the village whose owners have paid for them with money earned by picking berries on the Shawangunk mountains.

A third early reference appeared in 1892, when M.H. Pike described the region between Minnewaska and Mohonk in an article in *Garden and Forest* magazine:

The beneficent processes of nature have been constantly interrupted by fires that have raged everywhere. . . . The small farmers on the lower slopes, and the squatters hidden among the rocks, make a poor living by the harvest of Blueberries and other kindred fruit, and often have set fires to burn over large tracts because a growth of this kind follows.

The first major blaze of this century was described in *The Ellenville Journal* for April 29, 1904.

About eight o'clock on Saturday morning a fire was started on the mountain not far above the zinc mines, which . . . gained such headway and spread to such extent that it defied control. . . . The fire climbed the steeps to High Point and spread northward to "Shingle Gully," devastating a tract of from two to three thousand acres. . . . The line of flame traveled in circles, and now and then seizing upon dry clumps of brush or trees blazed out in great bonfires. . . . Nothing is known as to the origin of the fire, which was the most extensive in several years.

Another large fire burned about May 19-21, 1906. According to *The Ellenville Journal*, the fire started "up toward Lake Awosting" and spread through properties in the townships of Wawarsing, Rochester, Gardiner, and possibly New Paltz. Chiefly affected were the Minnewaska resort lands, but five hundred acres of Mohonk, and some other holdings, burned as well. There apparently was more than one source of the fire. "Probably 3000 acres [were] traversed by the flames," a figure that may or may not refer only to acreage scorched on the Minnewaska tract. Interestingly enough, this blaze was not blamed on berrypickers: "It is said that the principal fire was started where parties had been without permission cutting wood, hoops, &c., and very likely by them to cover the trail of their unlawful doings."

The Ellenville Journal for August 15, 1907 reported that a "very destructive fire" had started on the mountain the previous day, above the hamlet of Crawford in the town of Shawangunk, "and has been burning and spreading since. Wednesday night it stretched some miles along the mountain top, and down the west side. . . . It is burning over an immense area of the mountain."

The plateau of the Badlands burned over in a blaze of short duration, in the spring of 1922. The *Journal* for (Thursday) April 27 of that year reported that "Wednesday a large fire started on top of the mountain between Lake Awosting and the observation tower at High Point." The fire was fought all Wednesday night and was under control "about seven o'clock this morning." The paper states that "we understand it burned over a large extent of territory, covering practically the entire flats between the Lake and High Point."

A huge fire burned on the mountain from July 16-24, 1923. According to *The Ellenville Journal*, it started near Lake Maratanza and consumed six thousand acres. Mohonk records indicate the fire extended as far as Lake Awosting. The State Conservation Commission's *Annual Report to the Legislature* contains the following description:

> *The largest fire of the year was in the Shawangunk Mountains. This fire started on the top of the ridge in the section much frequented by berry pickers, and was undoubtedly caused by them. Starting at a point not clearly visible from the nearest fire observation tower the fire got under way rapidly, fanned by a high wind which got full sweep on the broad, flat mountain top. By the time the ranger and his assistants got to work on the fire it had already assumed large proportions. For many days large crews were employed fighting the fire, because it was extremely difficult to check it on account of the rough character of the ground. As soon as the fire worked down off the top of the mountain, it got into gulleys and crevices in the rocks where it was almost impossible to extinguish it.*
>
> *In spite of the large area burned, . . . the damage consisted merely of the destruction of brush which had grown up on land in many cases repeatedly burned over before.*

The conflagration of 1939 is one that assumed legendary

status among berrypickers with whom I've spoken, for much of the action was around the Smiley Road camps and picking areas. According to *The Ellenville Journal,*

> *Four fires were discovered almost simultaneously at various points on the Shawangunk range above the ice cave at 12:05 o'clock last Friday afternoon [July 21]. The blaze spread with incredible speed along the parched ground and through the dry forests and soon stretched for miles along either side of the mountain.*

At its upper edge, the fire burned as far as the Fire Tower Road, coming within a few hundred feet of the High Point ranger station. Wind-blown embers spread the blaze down off the cliff to the hardwoods of South Gully, but this ignition was quickly extinguished. Fire was roaring in the Witches' Hole, and Napanoch prison inmates were called on to fight fire near the foot of the mountain in that section.

Records in the New Paltz office of the Department of Environmental Conservation (DEC) point to two main fires during the week ending July 27, listing "berrypickers" as the cause. Around the Ice Caves, 720 acres were burned, with the fire started in four places, as the *Journal* had also stated. In the Stony Kill area (and west to the Four-Mile Post or Napanoch Point), 682 acres were afire, with three separate points of ignition. Both blazes involved surface, crown, and ground fire.

"Can found containing kerosene and rags," notes the report.

The Ellenville Journal had this to say, in summary:

> *The burned over area on the top of the mountain is mostly of little value, consisting of stunted scrub pine and oak. It is fertile huckleberry country and within a*

year or so, following this clearing of the land by fire, there will be bumper crops of the berries, which has not been the case recently. Indeed, it will be hard to make any of the old residents of this section believe that anything but prospects of future crops of huckleberries had aught to do with starting the fire.

The great fire of 1947 deserves separate treatment, and will be described in the next chapter. Following the '47 blaze, the next fire of consequence—probably the last true berrypickers' fire—occurred July 17-21, 1953 and blackened six hundred acres. Most of the area affected had been burned in 1939, and much of the lower portion in '47. The fire's eastern flank was held by a firebreak cut along the route between the Three-Mile Post and the fire tower. *The Ellenville Journal* gave the following description:

Starting near the Two Mile Post, the fire burned southeast about four miles [sic] along the mountain, a good part of the time against the wind, and ate its way as far southeasterly as the former gliderport near Maratanza Lake. Volunteers were successful in confining the blaze to the westerly side of the Fire Tower road and preventing it from spreading to the easterly slopes.

Volunteers saw a shape resembling a man in a raincoat at the peak of the fire Friday night making an errant path along the flat expanse of the old glider port.

They started to his aid, thinking he might be in trouble, only to discover, as they approached the shape, that the man in a raincoat was a large black bear. It fled without any help from the fire fighters.

Another fire ignited later the same summer, about five o'clock on the afternoon of Monday August 31, after a period of drought and intense heat. According to the DEC, 250 acres were burned, with the fire attributed to a careless smoker. Newspaper accounts give the area burned as about a hundred acres; an oral source suggested to me there were multiple ignitions by an arsonist who was not a berrypicker.

It would appear that the fire started near Sam's Point but that most of the acreage burned lay south and southeast of Lake Maratanza, between the top of the cliff and the Maratanza road, east to about the streambed that forms the lake's outlet and drains off toward the Verkeerder Kill. Much of the drama reportedly occurred just above the Sam's Point ice caves, where, I've been told, some of the fire fighters had to abandon equipment and seek refuge in and around the caves. Smoke poured down off the mountain, toward the southeast, causing a perceived threat to houses along Oregon Trail and the hamlet of Crawford, though in fact the flames remained above the escarpment.

The last large fire in the northern Shawangunks occurred early in August of 1964, during the dryest summer of the century's worst drought. It burned 1350 acres of pine barrens in an area extending southwestward from George Decker's place (above Rock Haven Road) to beyond the Smiley Road. Although classified as incendiary, it was not a berrypickers' fire in the usual sense. The huckleberry industry was virtually defunct, and although one or more former pickers may have been involved, motives remain speculative. The possibilities range from an attempt at destroying the large gypsy moth infestation in that vicinity, to employment considerations, to lingering nostalgia among those for whom mountain fires had formerly been a normal part of life. The blaze was fanned by high winds, and at times the number of men in service exceeded the availability of fire-fighting hardware. Water-bombing aircraft were used for the first time in a Shawangunk blaze. Operations were headquartered at

Decker's and on the Smiley Road.

Because of the drought and persistence of ground fires, occasional flare-ups continued for many weeks, as did patrol duty and mop-up operations by old Benny Tripp and some of the other locals hired as fire fighters. There were rumors that these flare-ups may not have been fought over-vigorously by the men, who thus increased the duration of their employment. The very last activity in the area was not over till about Thanksgiving.

In recent years, those who study forest ecology have begun to appreciate the role of fire as a naturally-occurring phenomenon. Nationwide, the long-standing policy of fire suppression has increasingly come into question, and here in New York, legislation now permits prescribed burns on private and state-owned land not within the Forest Preserve. The widely held image of forest fire leaving a wasteland of blackened earth and charred tree trunks distorts the truth, which is that in nature, fires more commonly serve to burn off accumulated forest litter, leaving the majority of trees alive. Decades of fire suppression, on the other hand, allow organic litter to accumulate like tinder, increasing the threat of a severe fire that could indeed destroy trees.

In the Shawangunks, the ideal compromise would presumably fall somewhere between the frequent grooming of the mountain by berrypickers' fires and the present policy of total fire suppression that threatens continued crowding of the pine barrens with deciduous growth.

Fire on the Mountain

Words and music copyright 1991 by Marc B. Fried (as part of an unpublished collection entitled "Shawangunk Mountain Folktunes"). All rights reserved.

(CHORUS)
>Oh, it's time for a fire on the mountain,
>'Cause the pickin's gettin' slow,
>And the berries'll do better in any kind of weather
>If they have more room to grow.
>Oh, it's time for a blaze on the mountain,
>'Cause the brush is growin' higher,
>When the berry pickin's slow, you can make more dough
>Workin' to put out the fire.

1. Sometimes they just used paper and a match,
   But they had more ingenious ways,
   Sometimes they used an old box turtle
   To set the woods ablaze:
   They would drill a hole in the back of his shell
   And tie on a twenty-foot string,
   And on the other end would be a burlap bag,
   All soaked in kerosene.
   (CHORUS)

2. The mountain burned over in 'twenty-three,
   They say the fire really spread around,
   And afterward the berries grew beautifully,
   As they do on burnt-over ground.
   It burned another time in July of 'thirty-nine,
   There's many remember them days,
   And there's many that remember all the cash they earned
   Workin' to put out the blaze.
   (CHORUS)

3. A bigger fire even was in 'forty-seven,
   It happened in October,
   With the pickin' season done the berrypickers had their fun,
   And the whole mountain ridge burned over.
   Now it's been many years since the mountain's been ablaze,
   And the birch and the maple tree
   Grow where huckleberry bushes and scrub pitch pine
   Grew as far as the eye could see.

4. (Three lines *ad lib,* fourth line *a tempo*)
   Now the berrypickin' camps have all passed on, . . .
   They ain't never comin' back, . . .
   And many grieve for that day . . . when you could get away . . .
   With bein' a pyromaniac! Oh,

(CONCLUDING CHORUS: next-to-last line *ad lib,* final line *a tempo*)
It's time for a fire on the mountain,
'Cause the pickin's gettin' slow,
And the berries fare well, they bear like hell
If they have the space to grow.
Oh, it's time for a fire on the mountain,
It's gettin' too overgrown for me . . .
But I guess many folks now . . . don't seem to care, somehow . . .
When they can sit home and watch TV!

(Conclude with four bars of music from last four bars of verse)

CHAPTER 3

The Great Blaze of 1947

THE GREATEST SHAWANGUNK MOUNTAIN FIRE of them all, the one that became legendary among those whose job it is to direct the fight against fire, was the post-season blaze of October 1947 that scorched 7405 acres of the range, racing through the hardwoods of North Gully and the slopes above Oregon Trail and Upper Mountain Road as well as extensive areas of pine barrens. It is fortunate that among the state officials on the scene was a man possessing both an observant eye and a way with words: Arthur H. Walsh had been with the Conservation Department since 1931 and was thirty-nine years of age at the time of the blaze. He'd been appointed district ranger just two months earlier.

In the New Paltz office of the DEC are three typewritten accounts of the 1947 fire. One is a detailed chronological report, unsigned. The other two are composed in a more dramatic style, being distinct but similar articles intended for submission to the *New York State Conservationist* magazine. They are both the work of Ranger Walsh. One was published soon after the blaze, but in severely truncated form. In the excerpts presented below, I have edited, reorganized, and combined elements of both articles and corrected one or two obvious errors. But to Art Walsh goes full credit for the wit, metaphor, and on-the-scene reporting that have preserved the story of this historic conflagration in such readable form:

> "Adventure," writes Steffanson the explorer, "is a sign of incompetence." This speaks well for those New York State forest rangers who never have any. However, dogs have been born with two tails, and black bear cubs do descend trees head first sometimes. We too had the unenviable distinction of breaking the rule. Now somewhere in the state there is a man wise beyond his times, and his powers of prophecy are mighty. We refer, of course, to the fact that he had the forethought to number this "District 13."
>
> Here is a country! It will have its own beauty to those who have time to look; some of us may go back someday and see. Hardwoods reach to the foot of the escarpment, but above, in every shattered crease and crevice of the Shawangunks, scrub pine has woven itself into a tangled thicket with an understory of dry fern and huckleberry—a devil's own playground for a fire and a nightmare to every ranger and crew.
>
> The prolonged drought that made a powder keg of the eastern states did not ignore us. October 21 glided up on us like a scalp-hungry yahoo—painted for peace, but packing six or eight tomahawks under his blanket. In an area extending from the Jersey line to the vicinity of Ashokan Dam, we were knocking ourselves out from October 21-28, trying to get a grip on fifty-three fires. Fifty of these we termed bad ones; what we called the other three is not decently a part of recorded history.
>
> With superb generalship worthy of a nobler cause, the incendiaries touched off the middle one first at Lake Maratanza, and then, when control forces were concentrated in a fight there, they smartly outflanked us

by starting the Ellenville fire on the west and the Cragsmoor fire on the south. Ellenville eventually came under control, but Cragsmoor and Maratanza merged and roared northeastward in an unbroken line through scrub pine toward the hell of broken gorges and canyons that form the crest of the Shawangunks.

The Maratanza fire broke out about one-quarter mile northeast of the lake on Wednesday, October 22 and was sighted from High Point tower shortly before 1:00 P.M. "This fire is believed to be incendiary—set by berrypickers," reads the official report. The fire burned northward, fanned by a moderate southerly wind. Crews were summoned and confined the fire to the east side of the Fire Tower Road. A fire line was cut from the road due east toward the ledges overlooking the Verkeerder Kill, from a point about half a mile south of the tower. The wind increased, and the fire reached and crossed this line before it was completed.

The wind now shifted slightly to the southwest, and the Smiley Road (east of the Five-Mile Post) and Fly Brook were chosen as new boundaries within which to contain the blaze. A fire line was begun from High Point eastward and northeastward toward the Smiley Road, but it is not clear if this line was completed. The crews worked through the night of October 22-23, but as it turns out, their labors in this area were for naught: A front passed through, the wind blew out of the northwest at increased velocity, and the fire ceased its northeasterly movement, moving southeastward instead, toward the Crags and across the upper basin of the Verkeerder Kill. It ultimately penetrated the Badlands only on the High Point promontory itself, in a fairly sizeable area with circular boundaries north of Sunrise Rock, and around the plateau's southwestern corner.

At mid morning on Thursday the 23rd, a second fire

started, at the foot of the mountain, close by the Ellenville dump. This was quickly extinguished by the local fire department, but either it flared up again or another one started. The new fire raced up the mountain, both wind and gravity being in its favor. This was known as the Ellenville fire. The small morning blaze was believed caused by a piece of burning paper carried by the wind; whether any berrypickers were involved in the later fire is not known.

This fire burned till Saturday evening and was eventually contained approximately by the streambed of North Gully on the southwest and that ravine's escarpment above the 1800-foot contour on the east, with territory above the escarpment burning from Indian Rock nearly to Lake Maratanza and from the Smiley Road up to the 1800-foot level and northeast to the telephone line coming up from near the Three-Mile Post toward the fire tower. Above 1800 feet in elevation, the fire's advance was halted by the paucity of fuel, since this was the area that had burned most intensely in 1939.

Meanwhile, on Thursday, shortly after the Ellenville blaze was discovered roaring up the northwest slope of the mountain, yet a third fire added to the men's woes: "At about 1:50 P.M. someone evidently thought the fires needed a little more help and another one was started, believed to be incendiary, near Cragsmoor. Due to the great amount of smoke in the area this fire was also off to a good start before we knew anything about it. The Cragsmoor fire added considerably to our problems due to the large number of summer residences in this area."

This blaze was apparently begun well below the cliff line, in the hardwoods south of the Cragsmoor-Sam's Point road. The wind carried the fire down the mountain toward Oregon Trail.

Thursday drew to a close with fire raging on three fronts. Although the northeasterly spread of the original fire had been curtailed by the morning wind shift, by nightfall this blaze was starting down over the cliff and into the hardwoods on the southeast side of the range.

On Friday the wind continued from the northwest. Most of the crew was busy on the Ellenville and Cragsmoor fires. The latter was now giving considerable trouble along its south side, where there were many buildings, and a large crew was working on this front. The Maratanza fire was spreading northeastward along the side of the mountain, and a crew was put in at Mud Pond to establish a line running south to Upper Mountain Road. This line was not built as far as planned before darkness set in, because a part of the crew walked away before the end of the day. However another crew began working upward toward Mud Pond from the road, hoping to cut off the fire below the ledges. Old lines everywhere had to be patrolled constantly because of ground fires.

On Saturday October 25 the fires began to burn rapidly with the rising sun, as humidity had not increased appreciably during the preceding night. The wind shifted to southwesterly early in the day. In the hardwoods of the mountain's southeast slope, the Cragsmoor and Maratanza fires had joined to become one. According to the official report, "The crews in the Walker Valley section were patrolling the line established on the south side of the mountain and constructing new lines around buildings which were located on the northwest side of a road which runs along the lower part of the mountain [presumably Oregon Trail and Jones Road, possibly Upper Mountain Road]. The fire burned within a few feet of many of the buildings in this area." With a tailwind, the fire above the cliff line, east of Mud Pond, was now at the southwest corner of Lake Awosting, splitting to both sides of the lake. Below the cliff, the fire line that had been started south of Mud Pond was lost from insufficient manpower and increased winds, so a new line was started from

THE GOOSE LANDS AT AWOSTING LAKE, OCTOBER 26, 1947. *Left to right*: Minnewaska owner Alfred F. Smiley; District Forester Frank E. Jadwin; one Edwin Gaiser and two other youths, unidentified.

Awosting, apparently following one of the carriage roads to Murray Hill or possibly Spruce Glen, then continuing southward down the mountain. From either Upper Mountain Road or, more probably, the tip of Sheldon Road, another crew was cutting a line up the slope. The men at both ends hoped once again to complete a firebreak before flames could sweep eastward across this line, as had happened below Mud Pond.

By Sunday morning October 26, with the Ellenville fire well under control and the fires fairly well burned out on the mountainside between Cragsmoor and Oregon Trail, the area requiring greatest attention was this eastern front, lying south and southeast of Lake Awosting. The official report continues: "The east side of this fire took on new life early in the morning with the wind in the south helping it along. The great amount of smoke hanging over this area prevented any definite location of the head of the fire from the air or any vantage point on the mountain. With increased wind velocity and the lowering of the humidity a new finger had developed between the crews, and the upper crew found itself outflanked by this front. Lack of communications between the crews greatly increased the job of coordinating their efforts."

Shortly after noon, pilot Fred McLane landed on Lake Awosting in the Conservation Department's amphibious aircraft, the Goose. He delivered needed tools and two portable radios that were soon to prove invaluable. McLane was met by District Forester Frank Jadwin. District Ranger Art Walsh, meanwhile, had left the mountain to meet pilot Bob Mason at the Montgomery Airport. Mason would be flying another airplane, the Waco. Walsh and Ranger Byron Hill had spent the previous day and night helping direct construction of the line south of Awosting.

Ranger John Behrens was now in charge of a crew on this same line, until forced to retreat when this line too was lost to advancing flames. Behrens and his men took up position on the crest, probably on Murray Hill, and were brought one of the radios. Walsh and Mason had by now arrived in the Waco and were flying over the area, hoping to make observations that could be of use to those on the ground.

We now return to Art Walsh's narrative:

> Over the fire it was impossible to see anything, and atmospheric conditions made radio reception poor. Then, suddenly, a harsh, cracked voice broke over the static in the earphones. It was Johnnie Behrens asking for instructions. Instantly Mason turned the airplane and began bearing his way downward through the smoke. The radio brought another inquiry, this one with a note of anxiety in it. The fire had blown sky high and Johnnie had led his men out to the truck on the shore of Awosting. In the thick smoke, none of the roads were visible to him.
>
> Then the circling of the plane opened up a hole in the smoke, and Mason and I saw something neither of us will ever forget: There was Behren's panel truck, like a tiny red ant on the shore of the lake, with little black dots swarming all around it, while ahead of it and coming from the right swept a line of fire six miles long, beginning near Walker Valley at the foot of the mountain and growing fearfully in intensity as it climbed toward the crest. Behrens was told to streak for Minnewaska, in language not approved by the F.C.C. It was none too soon, because as we circled back to observe the fire, we saw a solid sheet of flame leap over the escarpment at Castle Point.

Sunday evening a heavy dew formed over the whole area. It brought the fire down out of the tops and dampened the ferns and leaves. The next morning brought drying winds again. But the right flank of the blaze, having achieved its destiny at Castle Point, had nowhere to burn but downhill. With continued hard work, the fire was kept within a boundary running from beyond Hamilton Point southwest to Sheldon Road. At its apex, the blaze tried stubbornly to advance northeastward along the top of the Hamilton Point cliff and made it to within a quarter-mile of the power line crossing. The flames never penetrated very far above the Castle Point escarpment, where they were held with a firebreak of about half a mile's length.

The front from Lake Awosting back to Mud Pond, which had been relatively quiet since Saturday night, came to life again and broke away from the control crew. This was a crown fire with a good tail wind and threatened to go around the northwest side of Lake Awosting. Water pumps were used to drive the fire away from the summer camp buildings on that side of the lake, while a new fire line was rapidly cleared from the lake down to the Fly Brook. The fire was stopped here for good. This was the last outbreak of any consequence.

On Tuesday October 28 things remained firmly under control of the crews, who were employed chiefly in patrolling and mopping up. After a week of exhausting operations amid hot, drying winds, victory had been achieved. On that same evening, ironically, the rain began. "This is good old District 13, remember?" wrote Walsh.

The great blaze of 1947 has always held particular interest for me because of fleeting memories I have of watching the fire shortly after sunset from the back yard of my house in the Wallkill Valley. I was three and a half at the time but remember having the fire on the mountain pointed out by my mother or father and even seem to recall talk of berrypickers setting the blaze and then getting paid to help put it out.

When first I began hiking through the Badlands and Crags in the mid 1960s, I would often come upon solitary charred tree stumps amid the greenery, but I never realized these were relics of that fire, supposing them instead to be evidence of isolated lightning strikes. Years later when I came to learn more about the '47 fire, I began to keep an eye out for signs; soon I discovered that some of these charred remains were yet visible. Even today, the evidence is still to be seen, and not alone in lifeless form: On the mountain there are large, healthy pitch pine trees bearing deep fire scars encircled by years of new growth. The most accessible of these stands in the middle of the footpath that climbs the ledge northeast of 'Kaidy Kill Falls. Another rises from the rocky slabs of the Badlands' southeastern slope. They are veterans of battle and monuments to survival, aged but still vigorous. And they have a story to tell.

CHAPTER 4

Tales of the Long-Tail's Return

WHENEVER I TALK with people who have spent considerable time in the Shawangunks, whether they be former huckleberry pickers, hunters, or hikers or campers like myself, I ask them to relate to me any noteworthy wildlife sightings they've experienced. Thus I have heard the occasional bear or bobcat story as well as the inevitable tales of encounters with rattlesnakes. But the rarest of wildlife adventures in these mountains, the one that takes on an aura of legend and myth, is to meet up with that great member of the feline family long thought to be extinct throughout the northeastern states: the puma or mountain lion.

This noble creature has a variety of names, including cougar, catamount, and panther; the latter was often contracted to "painter" in country dialect, and seems to be the term generally in use during the first part of the nineteenth century, when these large carnivores of about ninety to one hundred fifty pounds last ranged through the Shawangunks as a matter of right. Since the time of their disappearance from the region and their return only in rare, isolated sightings, another name has come into use, one that acknowledges the single positive identifying feature without view of which any alleged sighting must be treated with a strong dose of skepticism: The animal has come to be spoken

49

of as the "long-tailed cat."

Former berrypicker Lillian Wood told me long-tailed cat sightings were not uncommon around Sam's Point during her childhood, until the time of the 1939 fire—though no one I've spoken to from the Smiley Road settlements claimed to have ever seen one.

The late Fred Martyn of Walker Valley told me of a panther sighting he made while hunting for "white rabbits" (snowshoe hares), about 1940. Fred was in his early thirties at the time. It was late fall or early winter, and the ground was bare. He was descending along the road, immediately below Sam's Point, and the cat, which he estimates at 150 pounds, ran across the road from right to left and down the steps where a footpath makes a shortcut toward the gatehouse. The animal then turned left, paralleling the road, heading southeastward. Fred told me it had crossed the road about fifty or seventy-five feet in front of him and was visible for a short distance through the bushes to his left.

John Stedner, Jr. was once standing atop the cliff, north of Sam's Point, and from his vantage point he saw a mountain lion below, amongst the berrypickers' cabins. This occurred during wintertime in the late 1950s. John went down to take a look and saw not only the pawprints, but also marks where its tail had dragged in the snow. He told me his brother George had seen a long-tailed cat about the late fifties or early sixties, somewhere in the Badlands. So I visited George Stedner at his house in Cragsmoor and taped his description of the encounter, which occurred during autumn. On a subsequent date we hiked to the area, where he showed me the exact spots where he'd seen the cat. At the time of the encounter George was in the company of a friend, Lawrence Keir, Jr. (who was no longer available for interview):

"We went on a walk before deer season, we were looking for deer territory. We went down the 'Kaidy Kill Falls path from Lake Maratanza, to 'Kaidy Kill. And then we came up the ledges, toward High Point. And we got almost up to the last little dip in that path, and you could feel that something was watching us. We stopped and looked around."

There's a little spring along the path, in the dip, just before the trail begins to curve around to the left toward the Split Rock. George and his hunting companion had reached some outcrops perhaps a hundred yards before (southeast of) the dip and spied the cat on an elevated ledge, about two hundred yards due north of their position. Because of subsequent tree growth, the ledge is no longer visible from the outcrops on the path; the area had burned over in 1922 or '23, and possibly as recently as the 1947 blaze.

> *That cat was standing up on that ledge, watching us. . . . It just stood there and watched us. Now, we walked into the gully a little bit further, out of sight, and walked up to that ledge. And we got to the ledge and the cat was on the other end of that ledge and he just walked into the brush. We [first] went up the path a little bit further so we could get in the dip, so he couldn't see us. And then we headed for that ledge. The only gun we had with us was a single-shot twenty-two . . . didn't know what we were gonna get into, either. The cat was a normal brownish-tan color. It had a tail that went all the way to the ground and back again. So it was a long-tailed cat. I'd say it probably weighed close to a hundred pounds or so, it was a big cat.*

When the two men reached the ledge they got a second look at the animal. The ledge is about sixty yards long, oriented west-northwest by east-southeast. The men came up on the west end and the cat was at the other end, whence it disappeared eastward into the vegetation.

I spoke to Al Smiley of Wallkill, whom I've known for many years. As a grandson of Minnewaska owner Alfred Fletcher Smiley, Al the younger (born March 1938) grew up summers on the mountain at Lake Minnewaska. During the early 1950s an older man (a hotel guest) told him he'd seen one or more mountain lions in the vicinity of Hamilton Point. "We hadn't had much sightings. Last we heard of was, Grandfather said well, in the twenties there was some discussion, back in the Trapps."

One August afternoon about that same year, Al was walking along the carriage road leading from Castle Point, heading back toward Minnewaska: "It was late in the day. There are a lot of places where you can get off the carriage road, on the lookouts, and get a good view, down off the cliff. I saw some activity there, and there was what looked to me like an adult cat playing with kittens—the way they were wrestling, their movement."

The animals were on the Hamilton Point cliff line, in low bushes, apparently right alongside the lower carriage road that runs roughly parallel to the road along which Al stood. The two roads remain consistently about a thousand feet apart.

"Did you see tails?" I asked.

"No question. I saw long tails. Now how many, I honestly can't say because they were off the road in the bushes. And then quickly, on their way. I thought maybe they had grabbed something. The motion was rather like a cat playing around with a mouse. But it was probably playing among themselves. There was a larger and a smaller."

"Did you see a head—a face?" I inquired.

"Yes. Came out, and then around—the larger one. Head, and belly, and then got up, and around and went back into the bush."

There have been more recent sightings in the northern

part of the range: In the mid to late 1980s, a hunter claimed to have watched a long-tailed lion emerge from a rock shelter and catch two squirrels, in the Sanders Kill area northeast of Route 44/55. He reported to a state park employee, Laurie May, who considered the description credible but did not learn the hunter's name. Laurie told me she herself responded to a report of puma tracks in the snow in that same general vicinity and is convinced that the tracks were indeed those of a mountain lion. Herb Florer of Kerhonkson saw what he believes were mountain lion tracks about where the power lines cross the lower road to Awosting. This was in snow, about December 1987.

The following letter, addressed to Dan Smiley of Lake Mohonk, is from a hotel guest. The letter is dated January 30, 1987 and signed Raymond G. Stevens, PhD.:

> *I would like to report an animal sighting which occurred as I arrived at Mohonk on 29 January.*
>
> *It was just about 6:30 P.M., dark with a starry sky. There was snow on the ground and roadway. Just after leaving the gatehouse, perhaps a quarter to a half mile up the road some movement ahead attracted my attention. When I saw the animal it was stationery, standing with its hind paws on the plough drift at the right side of the road. I saw only the rear half—I did not see the head or fore legs but I had the impression that the forelegs were on lower ground so the back sloped to the right.*
>
> *I am not certain whether there is a "deer crossing" sign after leaving the gatehouse but I know there is one on the way up the mountain from New Paltz. I had idly wondered how I would react if a deer leaped out in front of my car, so I was prepared to see a deer. It took a considerable readjustment of my thinking to realize*

that the animal in my headlight beam was not a deer. I finally realized that it looked "cat like" and then—still looking for a white flag tail I noticed a long rope like tail that hung straight down but did not reach the ground. My immediate impression was of the African lion tails I had seen pictures of on TV. I judged the animal to be between 30"-36" tall and the coat was smooth and a pretty "tawny" color. Both the size and the tail gave me the impression of "lion." I judge that I saw the animal for at least 4-5 seconds as I approached within about 75 feet. Since it did not bolt I wondered if it could be a domestic animal but it moved off slowly as I got closer.

Stevens examined a wildlife book in the Mohonk library the next day and wrote, "I feel quite certain that [a mountain lion] was the animal I saw."

Both the color and proportions of the hind quarters correspond with my visual image. However, the tail in the drawing extends horizontally and seems longer than what I observed.

I am not a trained nature observer but I am, as a physical scientist, accustomed to making accurate observations so I credit the fact that I had to revise my expected sighting of a deer to conform with what actually appeared to be an endorsement of the reliability of my description.

After a phone conversation with the gentleman, Dan Smiley made a notation that included these words: "Definite that tail long and not bushy." I wrote to Dr. Stevens and received a reply dated July 17, 1990 that included some additional information of interest:

> I might add . . . that before the end of that visit to Mohonk I encountered some further evidence of a large animal. Walking the Huguenot Drive a day or so later I noticed widely spaced tracks coming down the slope to my right. The snow was still over a foot deep in the woods but skiers and walkers had packed it pretty hard on the trail. The depressions in the snow off the trail were huge, and were unidentifiable as to detail, distorted, no doubt, because the snow was beginning to melt. A few yards beyond the intersection of the tracks with the trail they appeared again going down the slope to the left. Four paw prints appeared close together a few feet off the trail — and a mark as if made by a tail dragging in the soft snow bank at the edge of the trail! The next set of prints were at least ten or twelve feet down the slope. Again the fore prints were only separated from the rear by about 2', leading me to suppose the animal had been bounding down the slope.
>
> I attempted to impart this information to Dan Smiley before leaving but he was not available on the telephone at the time and I neglected to write it down.

In mid March of 1988 a mountain lion was seen by Jeff Bufalo, southwest of Bufalo Road, a private lane that branches off of Awosting Road (or Lower Mountain Road) in the town of Shawangunk. This was at an elevation of about 675 feet, near the base of the mountain.

> Upstairs in the barn I have an office. I was lookin' out my barn window and I was practising turkey calls for the spring hunting season, and I just happened to have a call in my mouth and I saw what I thought was a big hound, because I saw a big, drooping tail. When

it took a step forward I saw the head, and I was surprised not to see big, droopy ears like on a hound dog, and it was a tight, muscular, fat head of a cat. I realized what it was. I recognized it right away as being a cougar, but I just didn't understand what it was doing here in the Shawangunks.

There's a little gully and a rock wall, and it was just on my side of the wall, about fifty yards away. When I did go out and look for it there was some spotty patches of snow and I did see footprints, and they were large-sized tracks. The snow was only in patches. I followed it as much as I could, but there's a field, and when I got into the field the snow was melted.

Minnewaska ranger Bob Gunsch (a grandson of the berry buyer Paul Gunsch) told me of a panther sighting in the Millbrook Mountain area, reported to the state park people. From Herb Florer I learned the man's name: Ron McCormick, though a resident and native of Poughkeepsie, had frequented the Shawangunks since the age of fifteen, which is to say, for about thirty years. Mostly he'd enjoyed hiking or visiting the swimming holes, but early in 1989 he took up bicycling.

One day in March of that year—it was a snowless winter—Ron took his bike for a ride along the carriage road leading from Lake Minnewaska to the Millbrook escarpment. He was most of the way there when he spied an animal loping along toward him on the carriage road. He first saw the creature from a distance of about a hundred yards, partially obstructed by vegetation, as they approached one another around a gradual curve in the road. Ron estimates he was traveling about twenty miles per hour on his bike.

The wind was really blowing, so it didn't smell me. At first I thought it was a dog, and I said to myself wow, I don't see no owner behind it, I said, and that's the goofiest-looking dog that I ever seen. It looked like it was out for its morning jog. It ran maybe forty, fifty yards towards me and I'm still riding my bike, trying to figure out what it is. And then just at the same instant, he saw me and I realized that it was a mountain lion. It was like instantaneous, both of us together knew what each of us were.

The lion dug its front paws into the ground, turned around, and fled, still following the road. Ron's line of sight was unobstructed:

When it turned around, it got serious and was down low, I remember the back paws, that's what struck me, the tail up in the air and the back paws, low, sneaky like a cat. And then it took off. I didn't even have a chance to hit the brakes. I took after it. It ran, maybe, fifty yards, and then it was gone. It seemed to take a left into the brush, I can't say for sure because it was so quick.

It was as big as a big German shepherd, maybe a little bigger. It was thin, not like you would see in a zoo, and its skin was a little loose — at first I thought maybe because it was hungry or sick, but then I realized it was shedding its winter fur. It was definitely healthy, 'cause it was really moving.

Two reported sightings of lion cubs seemed to suggest the possibility that pumas had begun to successfully establish themselves as more or less permanent residents of the Shawangunks by the end of the 1980s: Ed La Forge, who lives at the foot of the mountain near Rutsonville, saw a female lion with its cub in the fall of 1986, when he was bowhunting in the hardwoods at a point about four-tenths of a mile due south and a trifle east from the center of Mud Pond. He was crouched in a ground blind about five or six hundred feet east of the Dwaar Kill, not far from where the old footpath approached close to the stream and the latter meanders through a nearly level area. He saw some movement down toward the kill, about eighty-five or ninety yards away, and first thought it might be a fox. The animal was climbing up and down playfully on the crown of a downed tree. He soon recognized it as a long-tailed cat, but was confused by the spots he later detected on its coat—only afterward did he learn that pumas are spotted when young.

> *I seen the tail bouncing around, and then I seen the big cat comin'. And I just seen a big, heavy tail and just a flat head with the ears, just a big, square face. And then as it got closer, probably within sixty yards, I could see spots on the small one. I could just see the big shoulders, and this thing comin' and I seen the tail up behind. I got to the point I took my knife out and I opened it up and lay it there.*

Ed doesn't know whether the animals got wind of his presence, but they disappeared from view and failed to reappear.

Muriel Heafy lives on the flank of the mountain in the town of Shawangunk. The lion cub she saw about dawn on July 31, 1990 was about the same size as the one Ed La Forge had seen nearly four years earlier, and thus indicates a more recent litter. Muriel was driving north on Bruynswick Road, toward Benton's Corners, and had just passed the Watchtower Farms' cattle feeding station when a spotted lion cub came out onto the road from right to left, perhaps a hundred feet in front of her car. It saw the car and darted back from where it had come. Muriel clearly saw the long tail as she slowed her automobile. She related an experience that had occurred the previous fall, that took on new significance after her sighting of the cub:

> And then I remembered I was riding the same direction, only in the evening, which was dusk. And this thing was loping through the pasture field on the left side of the road, headed in the direction of the mountain. And, you know, you think "deer," because that's what you're conscious of. "That's not deer." And then I thought "dog. No, that's not a dog." Well, by then I'm past, you know, and I kinda discounted the whole thing. But now I realize it may have been the adult.

There is a gap of three years before the next definite sighting that has come to my attention. This involved a pair of adult mountain lions, one only slightly smaller than the other, and thus suggests a mating couple: On November 5, 1993, Donna Pollard of Monticello was driving slowly around the Maratanza loop with her nine-year-old daughter. The mountain was shrouded in mist. They were near the northwest corner of the lake, not far after the road climbs steeply up through the escarpment and then levels out, when a pair of mountain lions emerged from the scrub on the right side of the road and began walking toward Donna's van. They approached to within ten or fifteen feet of the stopped vehicle, apparently curious, before disappearing into the bushes on the left side of the road.

Donna, who teaches high school earth science, is absolutely certain about the long tails. "the animals were larger than most deer that you would see," she told me. "I would guess maybe a hundred and fifty pounds. And giant feet—my daughter said they looked like they had slippers on!"

The most recent sighting I know of in the Shawangunks

occurred late in October of 1997. Jeff Stedner was returning at night from Kingston to his home in Cragsmoor, driving up the mountain on Route 52. He was about half a mile past the South Gully bridge when his car's headlights showed a pair of eyes, near the guardrail, ahead and on his right. The animal was facing him at a slight angle. Thinking it a deer, Jeff slowed his vehicle and then watched in amazement as a full-grown mountain lion crossed the road about twenty-five yards in front of his car, its gait increasing till it leaped onto the steep bedrock and disappeared up the mountain slope. Jeff saw the long tail clearly and estimates the cat weighed a good hundred and twenty-five pounds.

Whence have come these native North American lions once more to the Shawangunk region? Skeptics dismiss the reports of sightings or claim these are game farm escapees or illegal former pets that started growing up and were set free by their owners. These explanations might be likely in the case of black panther sightings, such as one reported from the northeast brink of South Gully, high above Ellenville, in August of 1997—though there are folks who believe a melanistic or dark phase may be occurring among cougars, as it does among exotic species.

The rumor exists that State wildlife authorities have been reintroducing cougars, wishing to keep a low profile for fear of provoking trophy hunters. The Canada lynx has indeed been reintroduced (in the Adirondacks) on an experimental basis, but not the cougar. The last known panther shooting in New York State occurred in the 1890s, with an unconfirmed report from 1908; these creatures are now protected by law, and any hunter who bags one would face stiff penalties, including substantial prison time.

The most intriguing explanation is that mountain lions have simply migrated back from the western states and Canada. The Eastern Puma Research Network, based in Baltimore, reports close to four thousand sightings since the group was formed in 1983; this figure includes reports from every state east of the Mississippi. One hundred seven sightings were reported in 1997 from New York State alone. While obviously not every report can be presumed reliable, it is also fair to assume that the majority of sightings by hunters, outdoorsmen, and motorists never come to the attention of the Puma Network.

Much of the East, including Ulster County, contains far more woodland today than a hundred years ago, when widespread deforestation had occurred in connection with forest-related industry and agricultural practices of the nineteenth century. Deer populations have soared. The gradual return of the mountain lion to areas it roamed before the habitat destruction and bounty hunting of the eighteenth and nineteenth centuries may therefore be an entirely natural phenomenon. Although sightings are not yet frequent enough to make the case for a stable, resident population on the ridge, there is no question in my mind that mountain lions have been seen here in recent decades. To observe one must surely be the ultimate wildlife experience for anyone who frequents the cliff-studded forests of the Shawangunk Mountains.

CHAPTER 5

The Verkeerder Kill Revisited

Among the chapters in one of my earlier books descriptive of the Shawangunks' physical features, one of the shortest was devoted to the Verkeerder Kill. Because the stream and its magnificent falls are well known and relatively accessible when compared to areas that border to the north and east, I had not felt called upon to write about nor even to explore this region in depth. In the early 1980s I became friends with some Walker Valley youths for whom the Verkeerder Kill basin was a kind of special haven and retreat. Through their influence, I have since become inspired to make up the deficiency.

The stream's name is authentic Dutch and dates back to the early 1700s. In deference to these venerable linguistic origins, I long resisted using the contracted form of the name that has been common locally for as long as anyone can remember. Over the years I've mellowed in this respect and now consider either form acceptable. There is little if any precedent for spelling the contracted name, but it makes sense to write it 'Kaidy Kill, preserving the *d*, so as to avoid irrelevant association with the name Kate and also to prevent confusion with the Kaaterskill Falls of the Catskill Mountains.

Standing at the overhanging rock near the brink of the falls, one looks out in the direction of Sam's Point and can not fail to notice an exposed outcrop, about six-tenths of a mile distant across the gorge, that offers promise of a spectacular view of the cataract. Other, smaller vantage points appear at somewhat lesser distances, to the right of the more prominent outcropping. With the help of a compass I found the latter. Access involves a rough, steep descent through talus and thick vegetation unmediated by any discernible footpath. There is a twenty-foot crevice here, a spacious outcropping of bedrock, and an unobstructed view of nearly the full height of the waterfall. But in other respects, because of some peculiarities of its location, the more distant features framing the waterfall are less visible from here than from the smaller, less prominent overlooks mentioned. The latter, which are from exposed talus rather than bedrock, are so much easier of access that they are to be recommended to all but the most unreformed of purists.

From the top of the falls, we take the footpath leading west toward Lake Maratanza; about fifteen to twenty minutes along our way, an oak tree of most unusual form presents itself on our right, our guidepost for finding the first lookout point giving a view of the falls. The tree's main branch hangs low over the path and bears most of the foliage, the crown having long ago disappeared. The trunk at the tree's base is highly elongated, its maximum diameter measuring fully three feet. But because one whole side of the trunk and most of its interior are entirely missing, due, presumably, to fire and subsequent rot, it possesses a cross section that is crescent-shaped (with the tips of the crescent well-rounded). There is vigorous growth of new bark and underlying wood, and it is this new growth that appears to support virtually all the tree's weight.

Immediately past the tree we bear left of the trail, following for a short distance along a natural pathway of broken rock before turning left into the bushes and heading due south. When an opening appears in the line of trees near the brink of the escarpment, we bear more southeasterly, toward this opening and another area of broken rock. There is a short, somewhat precarious descent (a rough scramble requiring strong legs for the return), but the final block of talus offering the view we seek is relatively level, and safe. The vista here is spectacular when seen at times of clear weather and high water, the falls illuminated by afternoon sunlight.

Above the falls a hundred yards or so is a much-loved pool of water referred to as the "Watermelon Hole" by my Walker Valley friends, who found these words painted on the rock when first they arrived. I had noticed the writing myself for years but never paid it any attention, since I usually consider graffiti an illegitimate art form in a natural setting. But the name is such a delightful one that, with the legitimacy conferred by my friends' usage, I began to use the name myself. One of these fellows was once inspired to build a tiny "gnome home," as he called it, among the spreading roots of the large hemlock that overhung the pool. While the rest of us looked on, he constructed a miniature house out of twigs, with dried grass for roof thatch and a finger-sized hole in the roof for a chimney. After gathering a pinch of leafy debris into a corner of the earthen floor, he lit a tiny, smoldering hearth fire, which caused a wisp of smoke to curl upward from the chimney hole.

Sometime in the summer or early autumn of '94, the long-ailing hemlock tree broke off near its base, falling across and into the pool. After what must have been a splash of cataclysmic enormity for such a diminutive body of water, the massive lower trunk reposed there in soggy ignominy, much to the dismay of all for whom this place holds special meaning. I wondered whether the swimming hole's sorry fate should be viewed as an ironical reminder of the abuse the great tree had suffered in the past, at the hands of hack-happy humans, or only as a reminder that Nature shares not a tittle of our anthropocentrism. My ruminations were soon rendered moot by the spectacular snowmelt, ice breakup, and flooding of January 1996, which succeeded in lifting the giant tree out of the water and restoring the Watermelon Hole to its former condition.

Much more difficult of access is another, shallower pool, at the bottom of the falls. When the stream is low in summer, it is possible to stand and shower directly underneath the falling water. As one approaches the cliff with the sun to one's rear, rainbows move across the rocks with every turn of the head, while nearly straight overhead, silvery plumes of water seem to leap upward from the brink of the precipice into the blue sky.

On the east the upper basin of the Verkeerder Kill terminates in a cliff face that marches across the crown of the ridge, parallel to the kill, northward and northwestward toward High Point. From the top of this escarpment there are almost continuous views into and across the stream's upper watershed. Several of these vantage points merit special mention. The first, from just off to the side of the footpath coming from Mud Pond, we'll refer to as 'Kaidy Kill Lookout. It commands views of both the upper and lower Verkeerder Kill basins, hovering above the point of their precipitous separation that gives rise to the great fall itself.

From 'Kaidy Kill Lookout a secondary escarpment is visible to our right, across an intervening lowland. This is the slab cliff forming the edge of the Badlands: It runs southwestward from the Smiley Road near the Fly Brook crossing for two miles to meet the top of the more prominent escarpment running south from High Point. At the acute angle formed by their meeting is a superb overlook that I call Southwest Point. The view is similar to the one from the lookout just described, but with a higher vantage point and the addition of a beautiful vista northeastward to the cliffs of Castle Point and vicinity. The view southwestward toward New Jersey is framed by the great notch in the mountain's main cliff line, where it falls away to cross the Verkeerder Kill. Close by, halfway down the ledge on which we stand, is a sheltered flat where often I've pitched my tent, and a little beyond, a large, rust-colored rock of glacial origin. The footpath toward High Point unaccountably bypasses this point for the sake of a minuscule shortcut, as it climbs up from the lowland to our south.

The third vantage point of special beauty is the most prominent and virtually the highest place along the cliff, noteworthy as much for its own dramatic form as for the panorama it commands. The reflection of early morning hues on its massive stone face, as seen from camping spots along the streambed to the south, is what led my 'Kaidy Kill companions to call it Sunrise Rock—a name I will not try to improve upon.

From here a certain elevated ledge is visible about 150 yards to the east-northeast, set back from the main escarpment. On a day with exceptional visibility, it is worth following the outcrops around to this overlook: There is a spot here from which, if one stands on tiptoes, one can see both Mount Greylock, Massachusetts and the hills about Allamuchy, New Jersey, points on opposite horizons that are 146 miles distant from one another.

Continuing northward from Sunrise Rock, the path immediately ascends and crosses a slightly higher ledge before entering the bushes. Soon we must leave the painted trail and bear left, following cairns along rock outcroppings, if we are to avoid missing some spectacular scenery. After a minute or two the path descends to the edge of the precipice and then bears rightward along the brink, with fine views toward the northwest as we follow along the top of this gradually descending escarpment. To our left, a final sizeable promontory juts out from across an intervening gulf. From this promontory, which I call Upper 'Kaidy Kill Lookout, a bird's eye view may be obtained into the upper basin. Far from the frolic of the Watermelon Hole, bypassed even by the footpath, the view from this vantage point has an intimate, deep wilderness quality to it that seems to invite introspection and fantasy. Below and to the right, on the floor of the basin, is an expansive, open region of terraced outcrops dotted with pine trees. There is a curious symmetry here that somehow calls up images of spirited Indian *kintekoys* or solemn powwows.

After crossing a small brook and climbing up beside a natural stone seat, the cairn-marked trail rejoins the painted one, which continues northwestward toward High Point.

On our next outing, we stop for a rest at the Watermelon Hole and then proceed northward to explore the streambed itself to its far reaches. Occasional glimpses of the cliff face just described will appear ahead or to our right.

The path follows the left-hand side of the kill above a narrow, shaded ravine and then comes back out into the sunlight at a pretty spot where the stream rushes down a curving slab of pitched bedrock. This place bears a strong resemblance to one other chute of water, some distance farther upstream, which has led me to start calling these the lower and upper Twin Rapids.

Not far above the lower rapids is the first fork in the upper Verkeerder Kill. The path crosses to the right side before the fork, then recrosses the right branch just above it. The fork is thus easy to miss. The left branch is much the lesser of the two in all significant respects and is often dry.

We continue upstream and come to a table of sorts that has been fashioned by perching a large flat rock on legs of stone. The trail bears farther from the main streambed so that it follows for a time near halfway between the two branches, in a region of sunlight, outcrops, and low vegetation. It returns to the east branch opposite a rock overhang commonly known as the Apartment. The shelter underneath is traditionally used by campers as a kitchen area, for which it is more suitably laid out than for sleeping, which is usually accomplished in tents set up on the flats above. I have memories of a venison dinner cooked and devoured under this overhang with my Walker Valley friends, one February night over a decade and a half ago.

Continuing up along the left side of the kill, we pass the upper Twin Rapids. Farther upstream we come to another stone shelter on the east shore. A man-made wall of rocks gives evidence of considerable labor expended in improving upon a natural stone wall and overhang. I learned something of the history of this shelter from Meinrad Broghammer and from Lou and Ray Quick. Meinrad, who camped at the Four-Mile Post on the Smiley Road, called the place Seager's Shanty (the name is pronounced SAYger). It was shown to him by his long-time companion, Blacky, who had told Meinrad of having first seen the shelter about the 1920s and of discovering an old axe head and the remains of a stove inside. The story Blacky had heard, relates Meinrad, is that a hermit named Seager had lived here through all the seasons for many years, about the late 1800s or early 1900s.

The Quick brothers, who camped at the Five-Mile Post among other places, knew of the Seager family but had never heard the term Seager's Shanty nor the story Meinrad had been told regarding the hermit. But Lou and Ray told me that Will Whaley lived in this same shelter through the wintertime, trapping, for a few years in the mid to late 1910s. This Will Whaley was also a huckleberry picker and once gathered 102 quarts in eight hours, according to Lou. Lillian Wood told me that Will and his wife, Laura, camped at the Three-Mile Post during the 1920s and '30s. She thinks Will Whaley might have been born about the 1880s.

Most likely, the artifacts discovered by Blacky had been those in use by Will Whaley a decade earlier. Blacky's tale would appear to be a garbled reference to the story of one John Seager, who apparently had a cabin in this vicinity at a time considerably earlier than the dates Meinrad mentioned.

In the Cragsmoor Free Library there is a manuscript by Le Grand W. Botsford that sheds considerable light on the subject. This manuscript is a longer, more useful version of the booklet published in 1902 under the title *In Days of Yore*. Information about Seager lies somewhat scattered in the various portions of the unpublished work. According to Botsford, John Seager was born about 1788 and had a home on the mountain just below Cragsmoor.

In reproducing the following, I have taken the liberty of correcting a few errors in spelling:

Seager's Cabin

There is no spot probably more wild or isolated on the whole mountain than here; [it] is, or used to be known as "Seager's flats."

It is in a mountain valley south-west of the Seager ledge and a little over one half a mile above Verkeerder Kill Falls, on the west side of the stream that supplies the same. Two or three acres of flat rocks there are, sloping to the east with small pine trees growing from between. On the westerly side and to the north of these flats grew the primeval hemlocks from which John Seager peeled bark, while from the finest specimens of the log he "rived" shingle; these were split with a knife called a "fro."

Botsford also writes, "He built a log cabin at Seagers flats the first roof being of bark, latterly of his home made shingle. ... The shingle made by John Seager, at Seager's Cabin, were of yellow [i.e., pitch] pine 21 inches long, and from 6 to 12 inches in width, and sold by count at one cent each. His shingles were extra fine, and brought this price ... in the days—'40s and '50s—when shingle were very cheap, [normally] selling at $2.50 per M."

The name Seager's Flats is still in use by Cragsmoorites, and I've heard the term from several former berrypickers. A wood road, which later deteriorated to a berrypickers' footpath, linked Seager's Flats with Lake Maratanza. Seager used this route to take his loads of bark and shingles off the mountain, the former to a tannery in the hamlet of Crawford.

Perhaps the stone shelter on the east shore of the Verkeerder Kill may have been used by Seager as temporary quarters while he was building his cabin. At any rate, I see no reason to abandon the name by which Blacky knew it: Though the precise location of Seager's cabin can not be determined, it would appear from Botsford's description that Seager's Flats lie just across the kill from the stone shelter; the name for this shelter might thus serve to relocalize the name Seager's Flats, which over the years seems to have become generalized over the entire upper Verkeerder Kill basin.

Some distance above Seager's Shanty the Verkeerder Kill enters a deep, swampy forest of hemlocks, thankfully regrown since Seager's time. The stream curves lazily back and forth, in no particular hurry to go anywhere. It forks for a second time. The right branch soon enters an impenetrable thicket underneath the Upper 'Kaidy Kill Lookout, where it begins to lose its identity to a number of small, seasonal tributaries tumbling down from the steep slopes that form the remnant of the escarpment. At the stream's fork in the hemlock forest, the left branch is the main stream and the one we'll follow. The footpath effectively ends here, for the forest is free of underbrush and easy of passage. Soon we arrive at the ruins of the "Plastic Shack," a large hunters' and campers' shelter framed with wooden poles and originally built by the Quick brothers and their hunting companions about 1959. It stood until 1989, was demolished by vandals, rebuilt, and subsequently burned.

At the upper edge of the forest, a five-foot cascade marks a distinct change in the kill, which regains its lively, upland character. We walk on the rocks of the streambed itself or in the bushes along the shore, depending on the season of the year. The kill bends sharply to the left and becomes entangled in a thicket, which we can avoid by cutting corners and rejoining the stream where it flows across bedrock again after a sharp right.

We arrive now at the loftiest swimming hole—showering place, really—in the Shawangunk Mountains, 1990 feet above the sea. We have climbed over two hundred feet since the Watermelon Hole. The water here descends steeply (though not vertically) over rock ledges, illuminated by sunlight. I call this the Little 'Kaidy Kill Falls. Little it is, with a drop of perhaps ten or fifteen feet, though some may take exception to its being called a fall. But it is a delightful spot and has no equal this side of the great fall itself and its nearby swimming hole, a mile distant.

Often I've been refreshed on a warm June day at this secluded place by utilizing one or another means to project the chute of rushing water outward from the rock, for a shower. The top of this fall commands a view to the east, where Sunrise Rock rises majestically from the line of the escarpment. Not far to our northeast is the large expanse of open rock outcrops that we saw earlier while looking down from the cliff top.

In the fall of 1984, I explored the wilderness of the basin to the left beyond Little 'Kaidy Kill Falls. On that occasion I had as a hiking and camping companion a young man I'd met while hitchhiking through Maine toward Nova Scotia, earlier that year. We followed southwestward for a fifth of a mile along the top of the same ledge over which the falls pass, then veered toward the west-northwest with the aim of striking another ledge, about thirty feet in height, whose existence I knew of only from the contours of the USGS topographical map. This second ledge lay about one-quarter mile ahead, in between our location and the Fire Tower Road. Approaching the second ledge, we passed through a thick stand of high swampberries in a swale that drains northeastward.

This ledge turned out to be, not a stratified cliff face, but a nearly vertical slab cliff, a geologic anomaly amid the gently pitched rock strata that characterize most of the basin. At the top we found a few berrypickers' cairns and a wonderful view that looks out over top of the 'Kaidy Kill escarpment to Castle Point and Margaret Cliff. After lingering to enjoy our discovery, we followed my compass through a dense growth of pitch pine and came out on a trail I hadn't known of that parallels the Fire Tower Road. I have since learned that this trail marks the route of a water line that serviced the machinery for the natural gas exploratory drilling misadventure of 1968. We walked north half a mile to the barren piece of ground at the site of the drilling rig, whence we turned eastward onto a seismologists' access road (whose location appears to coincide roughly with a firebreak described in connection with the 1947 blaze). We followed this bulldozed road to its end, crossed the expanse of rock outcrops described earlier, and returned, finally, to the hemlock forest and the Verkeerder Kill.

By the close of that day, I felt I'd finally come to know and appreciate the vast watershed of the upper Verkeerder Kill that I'd so often gazed down upon from the heights of the Badlands' western escarpment. The thickets of the 'Kaidy Kill basin now seem not quite so impenetrable and claustrophobic as formerly. The shores of the stream have their history, not least of which is the personal history that all can appreciate who've spent days and nights with companions in the camping spots and sunlit swimming holes of this Shawangunk Mountain stream.

A Kaidy Kill Odyssey

Once upon an August chill, while camped along the Kaidy Kill,
I listened to the rhythm of a merry katydid.
He sawed away upon his harp from somewhere perched atop my tarp
Until he lost his footing and into my plate he slid.

Round by the middle of the dish (as I was contemplating this),
He hailed me from atop a somewhat soggy piece of meat:
"Ahoy, good man, I've just returned to this, the land for which I've yearned —
Please spare me, for there's really not a lot of me to eat!"

Now katydid is just the thing to garnish chicken á lá king,
I know that if he stayed he would put flavor in my meal.
But I was curious to learn the story of his grand return,
And so, without delay, I cut the katydid a deal:

"If you have a tale to tell, tell it all and tell it well,
Keep your imagination from creating what ain't so;
Give it to me all in rhyme, we'll have ourselves a jolly time,
'Twill be my pleasure, Brother Katydid, to let you go."

He winked and tuned his harp a bit. I livened up the fire pit
And packed my corncob pipe with Cherry Blend.
He launched into a tale so strange, I sat and listened for a change
And heard one that I hoped would never end:

"It started with that summer storm, a year ago, if I'm not wrong,
It caught me up and swept me off this very mountain ridge.
I rode upon a buzzard's tail, survived the fury of the gale,
And landed on the railing of a Hudson River bridge.

"I jumped behind a Big Mac truck but soon was running out of luck,
Atop some golden arch I spent a wet and lonely night;
Then in the curtain of a hearse, but next beside a lady's purse,
Creased in a valise aboard a trans-Atlantic flight!

"And so I journeyed for a year: hither, yon, far and near,
All without a passport nor a number nor a name.
Customs never questioned me, and I always went for free,
But though I loved to roam, I soon got homesick, just the same.

"In Amsterdam is Vondel Park — I partied there long after dark,
Listened to musicians, watched the puppet shows they do.
I strolled the Yorkshire moors to see if Heathcliff's ghost would follow me;
In Irish pubs I found that I could down a pint or two.

"I passed a month in Portugal, but hitching was impossible,
I took the train to Spain but missed a boat to Tenerife.
Went on to Crete, near snowy mountains, in Iraklion, with fountains
Where the water gushes forth between a lion's teeth.

"I browsed in Turkish markets but they tried to sell me carpets
So I headed south, way up the valley of the River Nile.
I rode a camel's hump or two around Kalubsha and Edfu,
In Isna, after this, I had a lover for a while.

"I stowed aboard a freighter headed for the great Down Under,
I was seasick on the trip and then jumped ship in Sydney town;
Toured the Outback for a while, even saw a crocodile,
But I never could get used to living upside down.

"That's when I said, 'I'm headin' back!'; hopped a boat to Hackensack;
It leaked a lot and only got as far as Mexico.
I drank some water from a creek, was on the toilet for a week,
Went into debt and rode a wetback into El Paso.

"Was headed East at quite a clip; finally crossed the Mississipp;
It was here that I was nearly eaten by a toad.
In Pushmataha, Alabammer, nearly landed in the slammer,
'Cause I was from out of town, just walkin' down the road.

"Some Rainbow hippies stopped for me near Chattanooga, Tennessee,
I traveled with them all the way to Harrisburg, P-A.
They treated me so very nice, gave me hugs, gave me lice,
Kept me fed and played me Grateful Dead along the way.

"Another day or two went by, I saw the Shawangunks looming high,
Could almost hear the roaring of my favorite waterfall.
I finally found my mountain home, and never further will I roam,
It really almost feels as though I never left at all!"

That's when I wakened with a start—no longer was it very dark,
The eastern sky was readying for day;
The fire now was burning low, a soft and sleepy reddish glow,
The katydid, it seems, had slipped away.

All around was silent, still, except the sound of Kaidy Kill,
The myst'ry of the night forever hidden:
Whether it was all a dream, as to some it's gonna seem—
Whether katydid or katydidn't.

Part Two

CHAPTER 6

Interiors

WHEN MY CABIN in the Shawangunk Mountain Badlands was completed in 1967, I saw its future primarily in terms of a base camp for exploring the surrounding wilderness and as a cozy sanctuary for enjoying the Shawangunks during high winter. I was for many years more of a winter than a summer person, and the prospect of snowshoeing up there with a friend and sitting around a warm stove while the wind and snow held forth outside appealed to me greatly. I had built the cabin in solitude and felt the time had come to "divide the desolation" with companions for a change.

In those years, warm-weather trips were infrequent events for me. During the decade following the cabin's construction, my summers were occupied in various ways: I was finishing up college, or immersed in research toward my book on seventeenth-century Ulster County, or involved full-time in political campaigns; there was a return to work as a full-time musician and a summer's employment with teenagers as a wilderness guide/counselor in the West.

The original purposes for which I envisioned the cabin were well served during those years, and indeed continue to be entirely relevant. But both gradually and, at times, in discernible stages, my own relationship with both my cabin and the mountain have undergone changes: Beginning in 1977, a degree of independence and stability in my affairs of life have permitted warm-season camping trips to become a matter of annual tradition. And although I welcome suitable companionship during both these and my annual winter visits to the cabin, I have long since rediscovered the pleasures of solitude in the mountains and have ceased planning my visits around the vagaries of friends' schedules or moods. Solitude demands and also *permits* an increased dependence on one's own resources and those of one's physical surroundings. Thus there evolves a heightened awareness and appreciation of little things: the movement and music of wildlife, the flowering of wild plants, and all the micromanifestations of Nature within the mountain environment.

One particular camping trip marked a transition for me: In late July of 1979 I arrived at the cabin for a six-day stay alone, after three friends in succession had tentatively planned to join me, only to change their minds. The previous two summers I'd had good company at the cabin, and I was frankly resentful at my change in fortune. To make matters much worse, the weather was unrelievedly hazy, hot, and humid, and by the third day I realized I was probably destined to spend the duration of my trip in the same stifling air mass.

The boredom in the air exactly matched the way I felt; I asked myself what I was doing up here, whether the mere fact of being at my cabin in the Shawangunk Mountains was supposed to be enough to sustain me—and I could come up with no satisfactory answer. But in the midst of my despondence, the very absence of activity or stimulation was working, I am convinced, to bring toward the surface thoughts and feelings that had long lain dormant.

On the fourth day, my diminishing water supply mandated a trip to the Verkeerder Kill, the nearest reliable source during that summer's drought. It was a day I was not looking forward to, for despite the prospect of a refreshing dip in the pool above the falls, heat and humidity have never been my ideas of hiking friends. But a strange thing happened almost the moment I set out through the woods that day: I felt an immediate uplift, happy to be on the trail, after three days of lethargy, despite the uncomfortable weather. At the crevice by the edge of the Bog I spied a large garter snake and was gladdened by this sign of life amid the torpor that had seemed to envelope the mountain. I descended via the Lost River, where I'd not been in three years, and was positively amazed by its beauty, and puzzled at why I'd somehow forgotten to visit it for so long.

Downstream along the 'Kaidy Kill I reached my destination and was greeted by the sight of two green frogs jumping into the pool as if to claim their territory. Stripping off my clothes, I waded into the icy water and realized I was not quite alone up here after all, and that the two little beings whose home I was sharing today were quite suitable companions. Musing upon this from the bank of the stream a few minutes later, I practised at how I'd describe this humbling encounter when writing in my journal that evening. And it was then I realized for the first time that virtually every significant encounter or adventure or exploration during all my years on the mountain had a written component, whether yet actually committed to paper (as my journal entries) or only formed in my mind—and that I thus had an entire book already in my head that awaited only the simple task of putting pen to paper. During the ensuing months, that is what I proceeded to do, resulting in the publication in two years' time of *Tales from the Shawangunk Mountains*.

The other development that came about as a result of those six sultry days on the mountain was my decision to begin taking warm-weather trips in the month of June, when the atmosphere is cooler and more changeable and a water supply easier to procure. I remembered the diversity of weather experienced during my first month of tent-camping at the cabin site in 1966 and also the more numerous wildlife sightings that seem to accrue that time of year. So in 1980 I arrived at my cabin during the first week of June and began an annual tradition of eleven-day holidays that, along with six days every February or March, have come to form the major part of my Shawangunk Mountain experiences.

As my use of the cabin has evolved over the years, so, too, the cabin's physical appearance. On the outside, changes have consisted chiefly of a series of security improvements, while the interior has evolved gradually in response to needs, habits, and whims. Visitors who've sought and found the cabin in the course of their treks have occasionally left me written messages implying curiosity about the cabin's interior. These notes have taken a variety of forms, either friendly, humorous, or profane. To satisfy this curiosity, I shall now describe the cabin's interior as it appears at the time of this writing:

Just west of the doorway—to the right of it as I look from inside the cabin—is my cast-iron potbelly stove. It cost me twenty-six dollars in 1967. It is now a bit warped in places, with one small crack in its base that I like to think of as an expansion joint. The stove continues to serve me well; I burn mostly sassafras, birch, and red maple, and if the temperature seems likely to drop below ten degrees overnight, or the wind-chill much below zero, I make a coal fire before retiring. This has been the case more than one-third of the nights I've slept here during mid-winter camping trips. In 1982 I bought a new stove grate as a spare and spent as much for the grate as the entire stove had cost fifteen years earlier. In '85 I retired the original and installed the spare.

Inside the right angle described by the stove pipe as it turns to exit through the south wall, I have built a small wood-drying rack of quarter-inch wire mesh supported by two wall brackets and reinforced with a wooden crossmember. More wood may be dried and stored in a steel milk crate suspended from bolts in the rafters, just above the stove pipe. Various nails driven into the rafters are used for drying damp towels, gloves, etc., and on other nails nearby hang a blue kerosene lantern, a pair of black leather dress shoes, and my cooking pans and pots, one of which had the distinction of being used repeatedly as a potty by a mouse during the very first winter, when the cabin's stonework was not yet made tight against such visitors. Farther from the stove, mostly near the east and west walls, other rafters contain numerous nails for hanging a variety of clothing items. Years ago, a winter camping companion relaxing on the guest bed and eyeing the cabin's interior, adorned with so many items hanging from the rafters like stalactites, commented that it had the crowded, cozy, comfortable look of the tiny custodian's room that was his sanctuary and storage closet when he'd worked as a janitor for the Kingston public schools!

Another friend once made comment to the effect that those leather dress shoes hanging near the stove were stylistically somewhat anomalous in this rugged setting, though these were hardly his exact words. The shoes were among the miscellaneous personal effects of my father, who passed on a quarter-century ago, his footwear arriving at the cabin some years later. They are useful to keep here and change into: in mild weather when my hiking shoes are airing out (if the ground's too cool or damp to go barefoot), or in winter, to avoid having to wear my insulated boots when moving about the cabin.

They superseded an earlier pair of similar black leather dress shoes that had served the same purpose until they started to fall apart sometime about the late 1970s. The first shoes had also come to me from my father, though in quite a different manner: He practised dentistry from an office on East Fourteenth Street in Manhattan and had among his patients someone who worked as a "man Friday" for a wealthy business executive. This w.b.e., it seems, had a full-blown phobia about his own feet: He'd wear a pair of shoes for only a few weeks and then, convinced that they were beginning to smell, would discard them and buy another pair. And these were not just any old shoes, but were reputed to cost something like thirty-two dollars a pair in 1960s dollars.

The man with the phobia apparently would offer the discarded shoes to the man in his employ, who'd then take upon himself the task of giving them away to family, friends, and casual acquaintances—really a very noble application of the current injunction to "reduce, reuse, recycle." Thusly did the man Friday come to ask his dentist if anyone in his family could use a size ten-and-a-half, and thus did I take home a pair for the cabin, a bit large for me but quite adequate for the occasional use to which I put them.

On the floor to either side of the stove are wire baskets in which I store dry firewood. One was originally used for collecting and carrying eggs from what must obviously have been a substantial henhouse; the other was once attached to a bicycle's handlebars. The stonework behind and to the right of the stove contains a few small natural shelves on which I place a fuel funnel, my canteen of drinking water, and sometimes another piece or two of firewood.

In the southwest corner is a triangular shelf on which sits my water tank, made from a galvanized pail in which I fabricated a spout. To its side is a soap dish, and above, a mirror in which I enjoy the luxury of a shave every few days. Underneath, a waste-water bucket hangs from a large hook screwed into the bottom of the shelf. The old bucket's heavy wire handle has a comfortable wooden grasp, molded to fit the human hand. A white-enameled sink rests atop the bucket. In its previous life it served as the reflector behind a large floodlight of some sort, the tapered opening that held the light bulb now serving very nicely as a drain. I picked up both of these items for a couple of dollars in the summer of 1967 at a junque yard somewhere near South Fallsburgh, in Sullivan County; I was working as a musician nearby at Brickman's Hotel. Down the sink's drain hole go prune pits, eggshells, carrot cores, the dottle from my pipe bowl, and other miscellaneous organic litter. Ashes from under the stove grate are drowned in the bucket, cutting down on dust, before the vessel's diverse, liquidy contents are emptied outdoors among some bushes, a little downhill from the cabin.

Another triangular corner shelf is located above the water supply and is screened off by a small curtain that I sewed from a burlap feed bag. A swatch of cloth taken from a discontinued fabric book embellishes the curtain with a leafy, woodsy design in greens, blues, and gold. Sometimes a companion gazing idly around the cabin's interior, two or three days into a camping trip, will ask me what lies behind the burlap curtain. I can then proceed to describe in glowing terms how my glass-front cabinet at home in the valley, with its quartz crystals, pyrite, Indian arrowheads, and seashells, can hardly compare to the array of gems and curiosities of nature that I've collected over the years and that lie artfully arranged behind this curtain. Often my guest will take me at my word, and I'll watch him get to his feet, advance to the corner, and draw aside the barrier to behold various rusting quart- and gallon-sized cans with barely discernible remnants of labels describing roofing tar, paint, or varnish; also, coiled and not-so-coiled galvanized wire, a paint brush or two, mortar trowel, wire brush, a wooden scrub-brush that has never seen use here, some plastic bags, and bits of wire mesh, scrap sheet metal, and other hardware.

On another, smaller shelf on the west wall, next to the water tank, is a roll of paper towels, a small, screw-cap plastic jar containing liquid soap, a small piece of sponge, and usually an empty foil-envelope that once contained dehydrated soup mix and now is blackened to reveal its reincarnation as a hot plate. I place my cooking pot on it when the pot is set down on the kitchen table. The latter doubles as a writing table and triples as one of the fold-down doors to my three-shelf, two-door, enclosed wooden pantry, which in its entirety measures about thirty-six inches tall by eighteen wide. In this I store everything from candles to cocoa, salt and cereal to soup to nuts, corn oil, kitchen utensils, molasses, and matchbooks, tahini, raisins, and bread. Anything the least bit perishable is brought with me for each visit, with the excess removed at the end of my stay. Some of the food items most vulnerable to insect marauders are enclosed in metal or plastic containers obtained from a variety of sources and bearing printed inscriptions such as *coffee, flour, cream cheese and lox spread,* or *chopped chicken livers.* These labels serve the additional purpose of confusing the insects.

Sitting on top of the pantry is a small bag containing mortar mix, for patch jobs at the base of the exterior stonework.

Nearby, in the space above the corner brace that reinforces and joins the plates of the south and west walls, I store the window shutters and steel window shields when they are not in use. Suspended from the bottom of the pantry is a dish towel rack fashioned from the metal handle of my discarded stone cart of 1966.

One day during the cabin's year of construction, I had just finished painting the window sills, sashes, and jambs with oil-based primer and was looking about for a surface on which to wipe the brush. At home in the valley, the stringers of my cellar stairs and walls of the coal bin have traditionally been used for this purpose, and an unruly but not unattractive mix of overlapping colors has evolved. Here at the cabin, I saw no reason why I couldn't use the underside of the roof boards for the same purpose, since I was planning to insulate this surface and enclose it in plywood (to be nailed across the bottom of the rafters). So I cleaned my brush on a few square feet overhead, not far from this southwest corner. I subsequently decided to leave the roof boards unenclosed, because of the risk of moisture build-up in the enclosure, and also to avoid decreasing my head space by four inches. Sanding away the white-painted brush strokes proved a tedious affair, and chemical paint remover seemed too toxic and drastic an alternative. The paint blotches remain even today as a reminder of the folly of my impatience and lack of forethought, but I have grown comfortably accustomed to this minor imperfection and try to think of it as sort of a beauty mark on the smooth, dark-grained undersurface of the cedar boards.

On the cabin's natural stone floor stand two beds, one a light-weight fold-up cot perched atop stones and small concrete platforms to compensate for the ground's slant, the other of wooden frame construction, prefabricated at home and bolted together. There is a space between the head of this bed and the bottom of the north stone wall, which is formed by a slanting natural ledge of rock; in this space I store my snowshoes and crampons during winter visits to the cabin. This bed is sturdy and trouble-free and serves as a guest bed and couch, or as a storage shelf when I'm alone at the cabin. But the other cot, with its bedsprings, is the more comfortable for extended use and is the bed I sleep on. Sharing the floor space are two or three mud mats to elevate one's feet above the often damp bedrock, two plastic barrels filled with kindling wood, and another barrel for waste paper, which I use for starting fires in the stove. There is also a twelve- by twenty-seven-inch wooden table, supported on a steel tripod upon which a twenty-gallon water tank once rested. I set my gasoline stove on this table when I wish to cook a meal or boil water. At bedtime it becomes a night stand. Tucked away under the beds are jugs for water storage, buckets containing coal, a steel container with tight-fitting lid for storing empty tin cans, and in a cool spot amongst the water jugs, a container for perishables such as butter, cheese, bacon, carrots, and eggs.

The cabin's low north wall bears a large utility shelf with a variety of items, some that I bring each time to the cabin and some that remain. In the latter category is a catch-all box containing an impressive array of hardware miscellanea accumulated over the decades. On a few occasions, this collection has facilitated vital emergency repairs, such as construction of legs to cradle the stove grate when two of the three iron supporting tabs broke off from the inner firebox wall during frigid weather.

A particularly brilliant fabrication becomes a kind of palimpsest, in which the hardware components tell a story of successive uses, obsolescences, and reuses over the years. Several years ago I called upon this junk collection to make a repair of my bow saw that hangs above the utility shelf, thus salvaging my firewood-cutting plans during a winter camp-

My EPETRT

One of my most honored friends
Is my box of hardware odds & ends:
Of nuts & bolts & rods & braces
Salvaged from the oddest places,
Funky manufactured junk
From some contraption, now defunct.
Some device declared a goner
Come a kind of organ donor:
Eyes, & "male" and "female" parts
That screw, & pins & shims & springs,
Wires, wedges, widgets, washers,
U-clamps, hose clamps, rivets, rings,
Things round, hollow, flat, or phallic
(Most all of which are metallic),
Shaped like ess or tee or gamma,
Alphabetic panorama!
Buckles, wing nuts, spools from tapes,
Stuff with truly loony shapes
Of nameless geometric idiom
(Plain to see it ain't Euclidean);
Stuff so nice, you knew worth saving
(Stuff no spouse would view unscathing),
Miscellaneous & more, ex-
Traneous gizmos galore —
Ah, this stash, I know its value
Well. You ask why? So, I'll tell you:
Often when faced with a wreck,
This odd collection's saved my neck:
Fix-it man I then become,
From frugality or for fun,
Or when, a million miles from nowhere
Or from a True Value Hardware,
Something life-sustaining's broke
And fix I must, or fix to croak!
'Tis then I call upon my Ever-
Present Existential Treasure
Resource Trove (known to friends
As my box of hardware odds & ends).

ing trip: I was sawing up a fallen birch tree, late on a February morning, when the blade snapped off across the narrow bands either side of the extra anchor hole, near the handle end of the blade, rendering the latter more than an inch too short to be drawn into the slit provided in the tubular bow handle. Returning to the cabin, I set some lunch on the stove to heat and began rummaging around in my box of spare hardware. I took a small automobile hose clamp and anchored it near the end of the broken saw blade by utilizing a notch formed by the cutting teeth, after first passing the clamp through the center of a small turnbuckle from which I'd removed one of the two eye bolts. After loosening the tension nut at the opposite end of the bow frame, I slipped an S-hook, home-made from a large nail, through the remaining eye bolt of the turnbuckle and drew the other end of the hook (the nail head) into the hole provided in the bow handle. By retightening the nut at the opposite end, I achieved enough tension on the blade to prevent it from twisting during use.

After a day of sawing, some stretching occurred. By unscrewing the tension nut once again and unhooking the S-hook, I was able to make a fine-tuned adjustment without disturbing the hose clamp, simply by tightening the eye bolt a few turns.

The old saw blade worked to my complete satisfaction, and I continued to use it until it became dull with age, two years later.

Just above and in front of the shelf, a yellow kerosene lantern hangs from a nail driven into one of the rafters. This lantern I bought second-hand in 1977 from a friend who rented a room from me at the time. We had agreed on a price of eight dollars, half the cost of a new lantern as I recall. This friend and I had an easy-going household relationship that often involved one of us being in debt to the other for small sums, and for some weeks the eight dollars for the lantern was constantly being deducted from his debt or added to mine, until finally it came to pass that neither of us could remember whether the lantern had actually been paid for or not. We decided one option was for me to pay him four dollars, figuring an even chance that I'd already paid him the eight—which would have the lantern costing me either four dollars or twelve, depending. But we agreed that a better idea was to flip a coin and have me pay either nothing or eight dollars, as this way there was an even chance that fate would intervene and render the outcome a true reflection of whether or not payment had already been made. We flipped. I lost. Two decades later, my eight dollar—or sixteen dollar—lantern still pierces the gloom, across the room from its store-bought companion.

At each corner of the cabin, a triangular shelf is built atop a horizontal support brace that connects the sills atop the stonework on the two adjoining walls. The northwest corner shelf stands just above the head of my bed and holds my flashlight and reading and writing materials. The curtained northeast shelf is the storage area for kerosene and Coleman fuel, a gasoline stove, and two Sterno stoves. One of these I use frequently during mild weather, for heating canned goods. I usually set it on the flat cooking surface of the wood-burning stove. The latter, when in use for heating the cabin, can be used for warming food as well. The second Sterno stove is a double-burner unit given to me by a dear friend of many years ago who camped with me at the cabin on a few occasions. Somehow, to his way of thinking, if the single-burner stove was good, one with two burners must be twice as good. In over twenty-five years' time I believe I may have used it once. But I have no use for it at home in the valley and have gotten accustomed to its extraneous presence here, buried beneath the other hardware of the corner shelf. In deference to this old friendship, I have not the heart to get rid of it.

Above the head of each bed is a second, higher corner shelf, kept clean for fresh clothing or personal items. Above that the cabin's window screens are stored, or the windows themselves when the screens are in use during warm weather: These are tucked away above support braces in the same fashion as the shutters stored under the ceiling at the southwest corner.

At the top of the north wall, in the little spaces between each pair of rafters and between the wall plate and the roof boards, I store my dirty laundry. There are three small vents here that I close off in cold weather with the aforesaid laundry, though I leave them open during my absence. Small, hinged pieces of plywood, fastened with hooks and eyes, help conceal these storage areas from view, though if here alone during winter, I'll often dispense with such niceties. Two small vents atop the south wall may be closed off with small wooden covers. Even in winter, I open them when smoking my pipe or using the gasoline stove.

Each of the cabin's four main windows has a cubbyhole for storage both above and below, being three inches deep and the width of the window. The height of the frame wall minus the window's height is divided between the upper and lower cubby. The lower cubbyholes are rectangular in shape, as is the one above the south window. But the other three windows are in the side walls of the cabin, so the cubbyholes above are shaped like the cabin's profile, with slanting roof. Below each window are stored the nuts, bolts, and washers associated with window security when the cabin is locked up. In addition, these recesses can be used for storing keys, jackknife, and such. The cubbyhole above the south window is used for cans of Sterno; above the larger east window are stored a few tiny jars and containers, one with baking soda, another with wool yarn, a third with pins, needles, thread, and spare buttons. Above the smaller windows, near the heads of the beds, I store my gourmet canned dinners: along with various soups, such tempting delicacies as chicken á lá king, Shop Rite beef ravioli, and SilverSea jack mackerel, with some cans of pork 'n' beans (easy on the pork) for the occasional hot lunch, creamed corn to thicken dehydrated soups, and evaporated milk for cold cereal and hot cocoa. It is always a bit of a challenge—some might say fetish—to arrange the cans in as attractive a way as possible in these two trapezoidal spaces, starting with the taller cans near the south end of each cubbyhole and graduating to the shorter ones nearer the lower north end. As the days go by the cans become fewer. Like Winnie-the-Pooh counting his jars of honey, I take stock of my supply and plan my meals a few days ahead.

There are three full-length closets built into the plywood interior walls of my cabin, each with a hinged door that closes flush. One is on the east, with five narrow shelves containing a multitude of hardware and utility items, from nails, tacks, pushpoints, and Scotch Fasteners to sunglasses, spare parts, auger bits, first aid items, and waterproofed matches. On the door of this closet I affix, with thumbtacks, some of the notes that people have left outside my cabin over the years. The west wall-closet next to my pantry houses an assortment of old hand tools: screwdrivers, hammer, hack saw, pliers, wrench, and so on. A wooden yardstick, now in two pieces, bears the name "Chase Hardware & Lumber Co., Wallkill, N.Y.," which is where most of the cabin's framing material came from.

The other closet in the cabin's west wall has never really found a calling, being occupied by a few trifles that are rarely used and could as easily be stored elsewhere, if at all. Of these items, none has been quite so useless as a certain cheap, wire-mesh fly swatter manufactured by Lubbers & Bell of Clinton, Iowa. I purchased it on a whim back in 1967 and had certainly not used it since that year, if at all, until 1981, for flies and wasps have never been a problem inside the cabin. But on the fourth of June in the latter year, I suddenly got the inspiration to put the fly swatter to use *outside* the cabin. Those large, non-biting flies that often constitute a minor nuisance during late spring were worse that year than ever before or since. They swarmed around me and around various items I'd set outdoors to dry and were altogether quite noisy and annoying. So I fetched my fly swatter and carried it back up on the roof, where I'd been sunbathing, and whacked away till I was quite surrounded by the carcasses of dead and dying flies. I had hoped that after a few minutes of battle only an occasional zap would be needed to keep the peace. But after fifteen minutes of furious swatting, there was still no peace to be kept, and I gave up and sought refuge indoors. Like old King Dadon in Pushkin's tale, the fly swatter was not quite prepared for such activity after so many years of peaceful slumber. It hangs again on its hook in the seldom-used closet, rather worse off for its sudden call to arms.

Near the southeast corner of the cabin, a small brass poker and the lid lifter for my iron stove hang from nails that are driven into the side of the wooden bed frame. The poker is from Yorkshire, England, I believe. Its handle depicts a cat, back arched and ears erect as if it's suddenly rounded a corner to come face to face with a strange dog. I've always been fond of this poker, but unfortunately the handle parted company with the shaft, from too much flexing. Rather than discard it, I reattached cat to shaft with another automobile hose clamp.

On the floor of the southeast corner is a piece of two-by-four braced at an angle between the door sill and a cranny in the stonework of the east wall. This provides extra structural support and also serves as a platform on which to rest my hatchet, wedge, and a wooden mallet for splitting firewood. The mallet is made from a section of red maple trunk five inches in diameter and eight long, from near the bottom of which protrudes, at a comfortable angle, a sturdy handle, originally a side branch of the tree trunk. The knot in the wood's grain gives strength to this handy tool, which has seen many years of service. With the procedure employed, my hatchet becomes, in effect, a splitting wedge with handle, and most of the real work is done by pounding with the mallet, a much safer procedure than striking metal on metal and quite adequate for splitting the short pieces of wood that fit into my stove. This mallet, rustic though it may seem, represents a considerable advance in sophistication over the more primitive ones of earlier years, the irregularly shaped pitch pine knots with which I used to pound the head of my hatchet. The technological improvement that this evolution in my tool making represents is, I have recently been informed, roughly analogous to the kind of refinements characteristic of man's progression from the Lower to Middle Paleolithic period.

On the small southeast corner shelf are stored the sash or screen for the tiny window next to the door, and in winter, a candle in a pewter holder, to augment the illumination provided by my lanterns. In the warm season the candlestick moves elsewhere and its space on the shelf holds a small vase from Crete, filled with flowers. Above the upper support brace rests the bottom of a broom, its handle supported by a nail along the top of the east wall.

On the southernmost panel of the east wall, above the corner shelf, hangs the cabin's only picture, in the only suitable wall space that practical considerations permit. It is a framed, six- by six-inch, black and white, pen and ink print of the Presbyterian Church of Wetumpka, Alabama, built 1857.

CHAPTER 7

The Red Spruce Brook

I FIRST TRAVERSED the interior of the Shawangunk Mountain Badlands early in January of 1966, in the company of a hiking buddy of that era. It was an exhilarating day of precipitously falling temperatures, with a howling northwest wind. From the High Point tower we followed eastward along the cliff top for about half a mile to where the footpath begins a moderate descent toward the northeast. Here we abandoned the trail and bore off to our right, beginning a rough bushwhack of nearly two miles, southeastward through the wildest country in the Shawangunk range. Though I frequently consulted my topographical map, neither of us really knew what to expect.

At the time of this outing, I already knew I'd be building a cabin in the Badlands someday soon, but my thoughts were not yet formulated into a specific plan. The day's adventure was a broad, macrogeographic exploration of the plateau's interior for the purpose of obtaining a general sense of what lay there.

Three things stand out in my mind concerning that exploration: The first was arriving at some locally prominent vantage point and setting eyes for the first time on what I was later to know as the Red Spruce Swamp. I recall looking eastward, down and across, on a pattern of outcrops and small ledges that marked the swamp's perimeters, and identifying the general area from the contour lines of my map. Sometime later I remember our arriving by a crevice and large dead pine tree on the southwest edge of the swamp, farther downstream. Here we crossed through extremely thick vegetation to the opposite shore, turned right, and proceeded along the rocks. My third memory is of recrossing the swamp's watercourse where it was a frozen brook and of a momentary glance upstream, to our right, at a bit of smooth, sloping, ice-covered bedrock. From there our course took us southwesterly and then southerly, off the plateau. We climbed steep rock slabs rising beyond a beaver pond and picked up the trail from Mud Pond. We returned to High Point via the cliff line forming the southwestern wall of the Badlands.

Several times during the ensuing years, I had occasion to cross the Red Spruce Swamp or its outlet, always in wintertime. In each case but one, I encountered thick vegetation without a sense of any well-defined streambed. The exception involved a crossing lower down on the slope, where the stream was well defined, but an inhospitable jumble of icy rubble and thick, closely encroaching underbrush.

In January of 1971 a young friend and I snowshoed up along this brook from the Fly Brook lowland, after trekking there from my cabin by way of Mud Pond. It was rough going through the thick vegetation, and the streambed offered no respite. In the back of my mind was a hazy recollection of crossing the brook on that first exploratory hike of five years before: From this recollection I had a general impression that the brook had, or *ought to have had*, a more open section, where the water flowed directly over bedrock. But what we found seemed instead to confirm what had been my subsequent observations. Finally, when we saw the welcome rock slabs of the plateau's southeastern escarpment off to our left, we parted company with the stream and proceeded to these outcrops and thence back to the cabin. In actual fact, I had not rigorously followed the brook all the way up into the swamp. But in my mind I believed I had put to rest the vague, seemingly unimportant notion regarding this streambed that had derived from my impression gained five years earlier.

During the next decade the 1966 outing faded rapidly from my store of conscious memories, so much so, in fact, that I had completely forgotten about it when later I wrote of penetrating the interior of the Badlands for the first time in the *spring* of 1966, searching specifically for a site on which to locate my cabin. It was not until 1983 that this winter hike of seventeen years before suddenly took on a nearly legendary significance for me. For that is the year in which I discovered a glorious swimming hole in the Red Spruce Brook.

As to why it should have taken so many years to rediscover a place that I'd already had an inkling existed, I offer two observations: From where the water emerges from the swamp to where it plunges once again into thick, shady underbrush is a distance of less than two hundred yards in a watercourse of a mile's length. Furthermore, such a discovery would have held little practical value for me prior to 1980, when I began making early June my time for camping. For the Red Spruce Brook is a seasonal stream that ordinarily dries up with the arrival of summer. The actual discovery occurred toward the end of a hike that took me from my cabin to the Enchanted Forest, near the head of the swamp, then across to the far side and along the rocks in a southeasterly direction. Finally my day's companion and I decided to recross the swale and head back toward the cabin. To my astonishment we found a sunlit stream of knee-deep water. A short distance downstream was a six-foot waterfall, where I took a bracing shower and even washed my hair. A second, lower fall of about the same size completes the open section of the stream.

It was not long before this discovery rekindled my interest in another detail from the 1966 outing: the overlook from which I had first surveyed the Red Spruce Swamp. I was convinced that this was someplace other than the familiar cliff near the head of the swamp, overlooking the Enchanted Forest; for my recollection was of a more elevated vantage point, set back farther from the swamp's perimeter. So it was that when I noticed a small ledge and outcrop, barely visible above the pine trees about a quarter-mile southwest of the swamp, I became excited by the prospect of bushwhacking there and the chance for another discovery harking back to that earlier exploration.

Twice during the next year I made unsuccessful attempts to stumble upon that ledge, while passing between the Enchanted Forest and the cliff line and footpath that lie to the southwest. Finally, in June of 1984, I decided on a more deliberate and scientific attempt to gain the summit of what I had begun to call Spruce Swamp Lookout. These entries written in my cabin's journal describe my quest:

> Monday evening June 11—*The fabled (and perhaps mythical?) Spruce Swamp Lookout has eluded me once again. I started out OK, leaving the cabin at 9:10 A.M. and enjoying the rocky plateau north of the Bog. I easily recognized my destination, a certain ledge with a conspicuous boulder on top, at above 2120 feet in elevation according to my map. I was about four hundred yards from it when I got my last view, before dropping down into the intervening vegetation. I followed my compass faithfully, but when I got across to some pines and outcrops on the other side of the lowland, Spruce Swamp Lookout simply wasn't there. For over an hour I traipsed around the area, climbing trees several times, but could not find a clue regarding the whereabouts of my goal. Finally I gave up and followed my compass*

southwest toward the escarpment, recognizing en route two spots I had been to during the previous hour's search. As I began my descent into the Verkeerder Kill basin, I caught a glimpse of a doe meandering along the open rocks below, with a fawn following behind.

I am inclined to make another attempt tomorrow, approaching from a more easterly angle (and slightly lower elevation) and bringing my binoculars along for assistance. From there, win or lose, I'll follow my compass out to the Red Spruce Brook.

Tuesday evening June 12—*A very successful and interesting day! To begin with, I heard the coyotes yowling and barking once more. This occurred about 4:30 A.M. Returned to sleep.*

After a pancake breakfast I set out and again came within view of the ledge. I carefully followed my compass about five hundred yards westward through thick vegetation and came up on the ledge within ten feet of dead center. Unlike yesterday, I was approaching nearly perpendicular, which gave me some leeway—unneeded, as it turns out. I soon determined that my error yesterday was simply that I didn't continue far enough: I had been right on course, but when I came upon some small, somewhat elevated outcrops soon after crossing the lowest point en route (a dry tributary of the swamp), I foolishly assumed I must be far enough. I must learn to trust my compass more, and after today I shall.

Spruce Swamp Lookout is not the spot that [my friend and I] stood upon eighteen years ago, but it is a magnificent place, and will be an unexcelled vantage point for viewing Mount Greylock on a clearer day. There is a panorama of better than 180° that includes fine views of the Catskills, Mohonk, Castle Point, Mar-

garet Cliff, and most of the watershed of the Red Spruce Swamp. The outcrops and ledges directly overlooking the swamp are not visible, but there is a vista into the spruce forest in the swamp's upper portion.

From the lookout I followed a series of intermittent ledges and outcrops west and then northwest, adding my own small but strategically situated cairns to those of the berrypickers, and came out onto the trail bulldozed in 1967 during seismic explorations that preceded the thankfully unsuccessful gas drilling venture. I then returned to the lookout and ate lunch. At 1:30 I headed on a course just to the right of Margaret Cliff (114° on the compass), an easy trip because I had occasional views of Castle Point and also sighted on an S-shaped cirrus cloud that was moving slowly and in virtually the same direction as I. Followed along the rocks just south of the swamp and arrived at my swimming hole about 2:15.

The upper fall was virtually dry, most of the remaining water disappearing into a fissure in the streambed just above. So I walked downstream a bit to the lower fall, where I showered and kept cool. This has a large, gently sloping outcrop nearby, with shade available under a pine tree. While there, I took a good look both upstream and down, while standing in the streambed at the top of the waterfall, and realized for the first time that this was the very spot at which I had recrossed the brook, from northeast to southwest, on the same hike of eighteen years ago. A single cairn stands there; the spot is a logical crossing place along the route that follows the slab cliff forming the southeast wall of the Badlands.

So although there is continued uncertainty in my mind regarding the overlook from which we first viewed *the swamp, I had the satisfaction today of reliving that landmark outing by solving what had long been another mystery: our exact crossing point on the Red Spruce Brook.*

During the first few years of trekking to and from the brook, I established by trial and error a consistent course that made use of rock outcrops and avoided deep tangles of vegetation, while maintaining a reasonably direct route to my destination. Subsequently I made a small adjustment near the northerly end that necessitated a bit more bushwhacking but shaved a minute or two off the trip. Near halfway from my cabin to the swimming hole, I must leave a small outcrop and cross through a marshy thicket. The latter had often thrown me off course, especially on the return trip, until I erected a small cairn at its south entrance and cut a few blazes just deep enough to remain visible to the following June. Some years later, passing through here after a rainy spell, I placed three flat stepping stones across the little rivulet at the bottom of the marsh, to ease passage and mark the crossing point.

It would hardly be an overstatement to say that rediscovering the Red Spruce Brook has changed my life. It has introduced a new measure of physical comfort and pleasure, and indeed companionship, to my leisurely camping trips of the late spring season. The effects of weather and evaporation make this a changeable time of year for so small a stream, and its rapid fluctuations impart to it a dynamic that seems almost animate. The brook's passage from the sheltering confines of its principal watershed to the breezy freedom and exultation of its smooth, sunlit frolic—before its headlong rush toward anonymity in the Fly Brook's watery lowland—is a passage from childhood to youth, with all of the beauty and carefree indulgence that such a transformation ideally implies. The Red Spruce Brook has proved a faithful companion, its waters and shores unsullied by even a trace of the material refuse of civilization that so often manages to find its way to even remote locations. The only sign of a human presence antedating my own arrival is the solitary rock cairn I found near the lower fall. I have added a fire ring (when I slept here for two nights in September of '84) and the primitive, temporary stone dams with which I sometimes direct and concentrate the flow of water, and which springtime floods usually disperse with little effort.

This is the most remote swimming hole in the Shawangunk Mountains. The view from the top of the upper fall and surrounding rock outcrops looks westward, into the clove that cradles the streambed. Thirty yards distant is a large pitch pine tree of exceptionally pleasing form, with a full crown of foliage. Directly across the brook from this tree, on the southwest bank, I discovered an unusual pair of lesser trees that had suffered through a calamity but recovered and seemingly gained strength through their subsequent union. It is evident that one pine fell over against the second during a northerly gale many years ago, as a consequence of which its crown was deformed and the second tree lost entirely the top of its main trunk. They touch and offer mutual support against the wind, the trunk of the first tree leaning against the other at an angle of about 60° from the vertical. Both adapted by growing out from under one another, and both showed good health and adequate greenery, until the regrown crown of the upright tree fell victim to the heavy snows of '94.

After even a few days' absence during warm June weather, I often find the water level drastically lowered, especially if the stream flow had been robust during my previous visit. There is also a diurnal effect due to evaporation, as the near-solstice sun beats down on the swamp. I have witnessed dramatic changes during the course of a few hours, with the flow shifting entirely away from one section of the fall, as the water level drops. When the brook is low, often I must utilize a primitive gutter, made from a length of birch bark that has curled tightly in response to natural seasoning processes. By setting one end of the bark at the brink of the fall, weighted with a small stone, the water is projected outward eighteen inches or so and flows from the other end as if from a pipe. Often I'm thus able to transform even a dispersed, mossy trickle to a concentrated flow comparable to that of a fully opened faucet; under this I can cool myself to great advantage on a warm afternoon. When this arrangement becomes insufficient, I can eke yet another day of cooling showers out of my birch bark by repeatedly filling a wide-mouthed, five-pint container, with which I then douse myself.

When the upper fall finally gives up its water, I migrate to the lower, perhaps fifty or sixty yards downstream. By the

The Red Spruce Brook

Am keeping cool in the Red Spruce Brook
(If I don't return, that's the place to look),
Where it says goodbye to the swamp to show
The way to the Fly Brook swale below.

Near a pine tree standing tall,
By mossy, sunlit waterfall,
With pink azalea at his door
And leather-leaf along the shore:

That's where we two will share our day,
The brook and I, two friends at play
In cooling breeze and solstice sun,
As long as both of us are young.

If Red Spruce Brook knew where he's bound
He might decide he should stick around;
Though I know he must travel on,
True friends we'll be, for our brief time.

---

time the water level has dropped this far, much of the flow along the stream course above this point lies beneath the surface, relatively immune to the evaporative effect of the sun's rays. The rate of diminution in stream flow slows markedly. Despite the drying up of surface water flowing into the stream from the slopes of its watershed, a minimal base flow seems thus to maintain itself for a while longer.

Although the upper fall is by far my favorite of the two, the lower fall does boast a spacious outcrop and an advantageous position from which to look southeastward. My journal entry last quoted continues with its account of my day's experiences:

While I was sitting quietly and quite still on the rocks, a deer snorted and bounded away, from the woods across the brook and slightly downstream. Not ten minutes later, I heard a few indistinct snorts of some sort from the thick woods and underbrush below the ledge and downstream, on my side. Finally, after another five or ten minutes, I detected the form of a deer approaching. It stopped almost as soon as it came into view, twenty-five or thirty yards away, and grazed right there at that spot. For ten minutes I remained motionless from the elbows up, while I could just barely make out the characteristic movements, and occasionally, a silhouette of its ears, through the thick, shady vegetation. Many times I was certain the deer was looking directly at me, with ears alert.

Finally I grew weary of keeping so still. I relaxed more, allowing myself slow, easy movements such as lighting my pipe or changing position. This went on for at least another five minutes before the deer finally discovered me and bounded rapidly away, snorting loudly.

Once, not long after my great discovery, I was busily showering under the upper fall, my auditory senses filled with the music of the gurgling brook, when a sudden premonition came over me that I could hardly be the only creature to frequent this open, free-flowing water in such fine June weather. I had an overpowering notion that if I looked up, I'd find a black bear curiously watching my ablutions from high in the great pine tree of which I've spoken. I raised my head with a start and found no bear, only the sunshine and gentle breezes, for my audience. But I felt if ever there were a place in the Shawangunks where just such a placid encounter might occur, surely this must be it.

CHAPTER 8

Flora

DURING THE COURSE of the spring and summer, various flowering or fruiting plants and shrubs make their appearance on the ridge, embellishing the mountain's often somber beauty with color, texture, and fragrance, in ways either subtle or extravagant according to their predilections. Of the flowers I will describe, the one most unassuming in appearance is the most numerous on the Shawangunk conglomerate and perhaps the most remarkable botanically. This is the tiny, white *Arenaria glabra* (same as *Minuartia glabra*) or Appalachian sandwort, which clings to small cracks or miniature mossy islands on the outcrops, flowering faithfully from springtime through the summer months. It seems to thrive on adversity, gaining nourishment from scarcely a tablespoon or two of soil in places or growing in shallow, pebbly, undrained basins a foot across and scarcely an inch deep, its roots continuously submerged during rainy spells only to endure weeks of dehydration during times of heat and drought. This flower is a close relative to *Arenaria* (or *Minuartia*) *groenlandica,* with which it has often been confused by botanists.

Another small flowering plant of the Shawangunks is the bunchberry, a low-growing member of the dogwood family that prefers moderately moist and shady locations. Technically its small, yellowish-green center contains the true flowers. But

Bunchberry

*I wondered what she'd choose to wear
For springtime's flower fashion fair
(Such lacey pinks would be on view,
Such symphonies of shape and hue).*

*Beneath some branches, lying low,
Her understatement stole the show:
A simple, perfect, pure delight,
Her symmetry of green and white.*

*September I returned to see
What subtle charms awaited me;
Her flowery friends of springtime passion
Now looked drab and out of fashion.*

*I found her and to my surprise,
Scarlet jewels met my eyes.
She seemed to wink at me and say,
"I too need time to play!"*

---

the four gracefully curved and daintily pointed silky, white bracts framing this center constitute the flower petals in the subjective sense and, set off by four to six pinstriped leaves, impart to this blossom a formal, classical elegance unusual in a flower of such diminutive stature. The blooms are usually gone by mid June, but comes late summer, the plant metamorphoses into an immodest beauty with the cluster of red berries whence its name derives.

There are three relatively small flowering shrubs that I will mention in passing: The chokeberry is not a bad sort, its unexceptional white flowers with brown centers add just a touch of sparkle in May and early June among the huckleberry bushes. But its blooms will never be likely candidates to grace a vase. And its berries, as the name implies, are . . . strictly for the birds. The sheep laurel attains a modicum of stature as a flowering plant, though personally I find the small, cup-like blossoms a bit stiff and their particular shade of pink a trifle harsh. This shrub comes into bloom at a time when its much larger and more popular cousin, the mountain laurel, is bedecked with swelling flower buds of a much more pleasing hue that consequently rob the sheep laurel's blooms of much of the modest prominence they might otherwise enjoy. The magenta-pink flowers of the rhodora form large expanses of color in the month of May, the shrub growing thickly and carpeting boggy places on the mountaintop. But what a disappointment when the nose is pressed close in anticipation of the fragrance found in the honeysuckle, another member of the heath family, with which this bloom might easily be mistaken. For rhodora is devoid of any noticeable scent. Like the sheep laurel, this relatively low-growing bush suffers by comparison with a soon-to-bloom cousin, in this case the larger, showier, and divinely aromatic *Rhododendron roseum*, the mountain azalea.

    Words can barely do justice to the aroma offered all too willingly by this, the earliest-blooming of the Shawangunks' major flowering shrubs. It is sweet to the point of promiscuity, a description that can as readily be applied to the gorgeous and unreserved pinkness that permeates every particle of the flowers themselves. The only moderating influence—and then, only toward the latter part of its flowering period—is the profusion of light-green leaves, which offer a measure of visual sanity at the same time that they highlight the pink. As for the intoxicating aroma, no mitigating factor exists! Many a time, walking through the woods in late May, I have become aware of one of these solitary beauties before even it comes into view. Looking around, I discover the source of my nose's excitation ten yards distant through the underbrush.

The Queen

She's the queen of mountain springtime
But of royalty no kin,
With her perfumy excesses,
Indiscreetly saccharine.

Her exquisite pink caresses
Could seduce the very mist,
When her slender fingers beckon
Soon it's useless to resist.

She's a queen among the flora
But you'll fall for her in vain,
Though you'll see her and adore her,
You can never make her tame.

Her intoxicating nectar
Could entice the very air:
She's the Wild Pink Azalea,
Better handle her with care!

The blossom itself is of intricate shape, as are those of other honeysuckles: Five petals are arranged so as to resemble slightly the head and four limbs of a human figure. From the midsection extend five slender stamens with their pollen-bearing anthers, plus a longer, conspicuously protruding pistil. The entire arrangement bears a slight resemblance to a delicate, six-fingered hand emerging from a lacey, ruffled cuff, though more provocative metaphors easily come to mind. All too quickly, after the pistil receives another bloom's pollen from a roving bee, the flower's delicate structure begins to disintegrate. This fragility is also apparent when one attempts to gather some clippings for a vase, which I've done at times when the spring is late in coming and the azalea still in bloom during my June camping trip. The resulting arrangement never quite does justice to the shrub in the wild, which is where it is most inspiring and best enjoyed.

More subtle in its beauty and more tameable in the vase is the mountain laurel, which of all the shrubs is surely the most generous in its endowment of long-lasting floral beauty to the mountain. Coming into its own shortly after the azalea has faded, it is sociable by nature, growing in clumps or oftentimes large stands. The pink buds fatten gradually, until finally they burst open into pleated flowers of white or pale pink, adorned tastefully with darker pink speckles. A single flaw is the mountain laurel's rather shabby appearance when, after some weeks in full bloom, the flowers begin to wilt and turn brown before falling. In this respect it is unlike the azalea, whose blossoms are more discreet in their decline.

During the full heat of summer, when most of the other flowers have long since withered, there comes into bloom a large shrub whose lack of chromatic pretension confers upon it a dignity and graciousness matched by the elegance of its form: The rhododendron is usually seen in colonies along the shores of the major streams, where it forms a stately escort to the procession of flowing water. But its beauty is certainly no less when viewed from up close. The buds prior to opening are a rich pink. When the moment arrives, most of the pink disappears, and in its place are magnificent, delicately-scented, formal clusters of large, white or pale-pink blossoms, accented with markings of green. More than with the azalea or mountain laurel, it matters greatly which individual shrub is viewed, for quite often there are those whose blooms are sparse or whose leaves, so far into the summer season, are speckled with blight. But in a good flowering year and when in its best form, the beauty of the rhododendron is unsurpassed.

Some years ago I began visiting the mountaintop during July expressly for the purpose of viewing the rhododendron and discovering where it grows. In the Minnewaska region, with its deeper shade and perennial stream flows, the shrub is fairly common in places. To the southwest, the higher and dryer terrain makes the rhododendron more exceptional. The Verkeerder Kill has a number of these shrubs between the top of the falls and the lower Twin Rapids, several minutes above. Farther upstream the shrub is scarce; I found the last specimen in a sandy bend of the kill near the lower end of the hemlock forest.

Three Ladies of the Woods

This lady casts her spell in May
But all too quickly slips away.
As fair as any sweet sixteen,
She's dressed in candy pink and green
With honeysweet perfume; alas,
Of this she wearies soon and fast
Removes her lovely clothes
To seek anonymous repose.

The second lady's more mature,
She dresses with refined allure
In ruffled white and just a touch
Of pink, but never with too much.
Somewhere beneath a shady tree,
With friends as beautiful as she,
You'll find her in the month of June,
Summertime arriving soon.

Reclining quietly by a stream,
Her velvet shades of deepest green
Form cushions 'neath her pearly white:
A crystal chandelier of light
Or bright star in a summer sky.
She shows her beauty in July
With elegant simplicity.
This lady's finest of the three!

The Red Spruce Swamp has none, Shingle Gully some, and the Witches' Hole a great quantity. But the most accessible display occurs along the Stony Kill, beginning fifteen or twenty minutes below the Smiley Road crossing and increasing in abundance downstream, until the shores of the Stony Kill fairly exult in rhododendron as one approaches the falls. This is my preferred destination during the flowering season, when the sight of these graceful shrubs may be enjoyed from the cool refuge of a pleasant swimming hole.

There is a special event that occurs every year in the Shawangunks, beginning after the rhododendron has faded and reaching a climax just as the swampberries are maturing into full ripeness. It is almost more in the nature of a floral show than a flowering season, and has always been held at Lake Awosting, for as far back as anyone can remember. Although a few individuals have been seen exhibiting along the Peters Kill and the lowermost reaches of its foremost tributary, and also at the northeast cove of Mud Pond, these rebels (or stragglers) are only a tiny fraction of those in attendance: The vast majority will congregate along the Awosting shore for an annual monanthous olfactory extravaganza starring the snowy-spiked *Clethra alnifolia,* or sweet pepperbush.

The aroma of this flowering shrub is almost in a class with that of the pink azalea. But whereas the azalea is a delicate, lonesome beauty, the sweet pepperbush crowds around its chosen benefactor in such unrestrained and indeed weedy abundance that the air is filled with its delicious fragrance, which may be enjoyed in a kind of aesthetic harmony with the gentle lapping of Awosting waves and a cooling breeze wafting off the water in refreshing mitigation of the August heat.

This is the last-blooming of the major flowering shrubs of the Shawangunk Mountains. But simultaneously with the magnificent display at Lake Awosting, a more subtle transformation is taking place in the marshes and bogs not far to the southwest, in and about the lowlands of the Fly Brook. Here the Virginia cotton grass has become a soft, tawny delight of sensuous beauty, reminiscent of nothing so much as kitten fur, with an understory of northern yellow-eyed grass for companionship; while nearby, the glossy, chartreuse spheres of *Vaccinium macrocarpon* are beginning to take on a blush of pink, as they float in inch-deep water or lie about on their soft, damp pillows of sphagnum moss.

As the days grow shorter and August turns to autumn, the kitten fur turns ghostly white. The glossy spheres ripen to a lustrous maroon-red, and the sphagnum turns a sugary pink. How to tell when it's time to return for the harvest? When these exquisite hues are fringed by the bright colors of autumn foliage at their peak of intensity.

Wild Cranberries

Over mosses softly stepping,
Sphagnum spongy underneath,
Where the wetland sedge is spreading
Cottonheads of spectral wisp —

Solitary occupation,
Silent as a meditation,
Simple as repeating motion,
Bowing down to gather this:

Beads of burgundy here waiting,
Pearly circles in the mist,
Sauce to be, free for the taking —
How should I resist?

CHAPTER 9

Fauna

W<small>HEN PICKING HUCKLEBERRIES</small>, I've noticed, on occasion, a small but distinctively colored bug fleeing across the palm of my hand, having apparently lain hidden amongst a cluster of fruit until I'd disturbed his repose. Sometimes I've found one by itself, sometimes a few together, often of varying sizes, as if I'd come upon a family with children. I described the insect to former berrypicker Nina Addis, and she said, "Oh, you mean the stink bug; we always just called 'em stink bugs." Well, I was not quite satisfied with this answer, for though I'd occasionally experienced a faint, disagreeable odor among huckleberries, I'd never associated it with this bug or indeed with any specific source. Furthermore, it seemed possible such a folksy moniker could be borne by more than one kind of insect. So the next year I made a precise drawing of a captured specimen and brought my inquiry to a professor of biology at the state college in New Paltz. He wrote me soon afterward that he'd identified the insect as being of the Hemiptera order and Pentatomidae family, the specific genus and species being *Perillus bioculatus* — more commonly known as the stink bug!

Far more numerous than stink bugs are the tiny snow fleas that appear quite miraculously in the dead of winter, hopping about on the surface of the snow. I had noticed these now and then over the years, but never paid them much attention until a recent March camping trip, when I arrived on snowshoes for several days at my cabin to discover the mountaintop everywhere covered with untold zillions of these creatures. After a few days, the temperature, which had touched zero on my first night, soared into the forties, with a bright sun and calm wind; I found myself sunbathing in front of my cabin door, where these insects hopped over my bare feet and shared the foam pad on which I sat, neither carnivorous in appetite nor even a minor nuisance, since they stayed close to the ground and did not go crawling or clinging anywhere they might not be appreciated. Soon I acknowledged them as the closest thing to animate companionship that I was likely to have during the better part of a week. I became intensely curious about them, for although I've since learned something concerning their life cycle and how they earn a living (they dine on pollen, fungus spores, and tiny fragments of decomposing vegetation atop the snow and in the soil), to all appearances they had nothing more pressing to do than hang out and frolic about in the snow.

Before I was half through composing it, the little poem I wrote on that occasion had become more like a song of sorts, taking on a popular form that was wholly unforeseen:

Snow FLEAS, so PLEASE, tell me some: Where you from?
And how come you just appear when the year is young,
In the snow, in the sun, nearly everywhere I look,
'Bout a billion to the ton, you're really one for the book.

Snow FLEAS, so PLEASE, tell me all: who you be,
What you eat, where you sleep, you're a small mystery.
You don't stop for a chew like a flea on a dog,
You just hop 'cause you wanna be like a frog —

Say "CHEESE," snow fleas, I'll take a photograph of you
'Cause I know you hafta go when the wintertime is through,
So long, snow fleas, I'll be missin' you too,
Sleep tight, snow fleas, I'll be writin' 'bout you.

An insect that seems, according to my own experience, to have established itself in the Shawangunk pine barrens fairly recently, is the much-despised deerfly. I can not ever remember being bothered by one of these delta-winged devils until 1987, when they suddenly arrived in significant numbers. In subsequent years they have not been as numerous, but they've by no means been absent, and I can now generally count on their scoring a couple of direct hits on my person during the course of a June camping trip. Whenever one starts circling rapidly and noisily above my head in characteristic and inimitably infuriating fashion, I keep it moving with my right hand while holding my left fist clenched some distance in front of my left eye, tilted at an angle toward me. If I'm lucky, the deerfly will tire before I do and mistake the back of my left hand for a convenient resting place. I then attack instantly with my right and sometimes nab him.

If I'm not quite as quick as he, the near miss will nevertheless usually give me two minutes of peace while my antagonist cools his heels, contemplating his close brush with death; sometimes it thus seems as if I can't really lose with a good swat, whether I get him or not. If I'm quicker than he is and manage to knock him dead, I can generally count on about two minutes' respite before his neighbor discovers me and arrives on the scene, intent on avenging his companion's death; so sometimes it seems as if I can't really win.

If the mountain's flora is one source of its beauty, its fauna, deerflies notwithstanding, is certainly no less a subject of interest. In an earlier published account, I described the song of the towhee or chewink and made comment concerning the abundance of both the bird and its two characteristic voices in the vicinity of my cabin. A friend who is knowledgeable about Shawangunk wildlife related to me that the towhee always seemed to him to be singing, "Drink . . . your tea," and that this was the standard interpretation or description of the song that he'd grown up with. Now one thing one learns to appreciate after enough time spent listening to bird songs is the wonderful variety among the voices of different individuals of the same species, whose songs often display scarcely fewer peculiarities of tone and timbre than do the utterances of human beings, and often considerably more variety in content. But as I continued to listen to the towhee, I had to agree that quite often it seemed to be saying just what my friend said it was. So I wrote him a little ditty that began thus:

Perhaps the aromatic tea
That comes from the sassafras tree's
The one that's often urged on us
By Shawangunk's neighborly towhee

The second verse of the poem related to something this friend had corrected me on concerning Shawangunk flora, and is in the nature of a private joke. But I always intended to write an alternate verse to complete a little poem about the towhee.

One hot, sunny day, as I was following shady spots here and there about my front yard, I had the good fortune to be visited by a pair of towhees, or chewinks as I should properly call them in this context, who hopped about playfully on the edge of the outcrop or rustled in the leaves a short way into the woods, undaunted by my presence. At one point, one of them even approached to within five yards, apparently motivated by curiosity, and I remember wishing I'd had some bread with me to see if I could lure him closer. Thus occupied, the birds' constant call was "wrink!" or "dwrink!," rather than the characteristic towhee song, and soon it occurred to me to imagine that these mischievous playmates were trying to lure *me*, chirping out an invitation to join them for a hellbender off in the shade of the thicket. And thus was born the other half to my poem, which in its entirety, goes like this:

Perhaps the aromatic tea
That comes from the sassafras tree's
The one that's often urged on us
By Shawangunk's neighborly towhee;

No doubt it's somewhat stronger drink
He has in mind, when the chewink
Invites us from off in the bush
To stop on by for a DOOWRRINK!

A common song of the Shawangunk pine barrens, if it can be called a song, is that of the yellowthroat, whose call is so insistent and repetitive that it would almost become annoying, were this pretty bird's voice not so sweet—which makes the call rather comical instead. Some individuals sound as if they are querying, "Whadyado? Whadyado? Whadyado?" But usually the song sounds more like "Wichita! Wichita! Wichita!"—which inspired me to write this poem, which I call, *Advice to the Yellowthroat:*

Oh Yellowthroat, why must you sing
Incessantly of just one thing?
Such virtuosity in service to obsession:
Your devotion
To some crummy cow town in the state
Of Dorothy and Dole!

With your sweet face and voice cherubic,
Praise someplace that's more exotic:
Sing of Sanibel, Havana,
Or Sevastopol.

A yellowthroat that I once chanced
To meet perched on a pepperidge branch;
It listened to me very nice
As I delivered my advice,

Then cocked its head as if to say,
"Imagine that"; and then, away
It went. But from some yonder tree
It sent its answer back to me.

Not so unexpectedly,
The gist of what it said was . . .
"Wichita! Wichita! Wichita! Wichita!
Wichita!"

For several years I enjoyed the most exquisite of songs from the hermit thrush, about whom I've also previously written. I've taken the liberty of arranging the several elements of his tune in a sequence I found most pleasing, though in nature the composer was perfectly content to perform these elements in a random fashion. So although it would be mathematically improbable to hear the song in precisely the sequence illustrated, all of the melodic components (of one measure each) are sub-melodies that I've heard from this

woodland virtuoso.

One year I returned to my cabin to find that, although the music of the thrush yet permeated the mountain air, the tune had changed. It was then I realized that the particular melody I'd come to love was the performance of a single resident individual, now departed, and not something I could expect to hear from another member of the same species. So although lovely music yet resounds through the pine woods surrounding my cabin, it is a different song, equally beautiful in timbre but somewhat less inspired melodically.

To the hermit thrush I owe one of my more interesting encounters with a deer. It occurred just outside my cabin during early evening twilight in June of 1983 and was occasioned by my having turned around on the rock upon which I was seated, in order to more easily listen to a hermit thrush that was serenading me from the wood just to the west. Within half a minute, I heard the sound of stone against stone, obviously coming from a place on the outcrop a very short distance from where I sat. Since I was already facing directly toward the sound, I was able to remain motionless and await whatever was to appear. A few seconds later a large deer emerged from behind some intervening pine scrub, meandering along fifty feet from me in plain view. Its eyes wandered over in my direction; it perked up its ears, twitching its nose. Our eyes were in contact. Satisfied that I was inanimate, the deer resumed its laid-back stroll. After another couple of steps it stared at me again, but once more continued along, reassured.

Soon it was as close as it was bound to pass, on its tangential course; I spoke up softly, saying, "I'm not gonna hurt you." This, of course, was asking too much: It turned my way again, fully alert, then ran off with a snort in the direction toward which it was already headed, though not so quickly as to suggest it was truly fearful.

This encounter contained all the properly-sequenced elements of what I have come to think of as the "perfect" or "classic" wildlife sighting, to wit: First, hear the animal before it hears or sees you; anticipate its appearance. Second, watch the animal come in sight. Third, identify it while it is still in clear view. Fourth, anticipate and witness its discovery of you. Fifth, make eye contact with the animal and observe its response. There was, in addition, the added novelty of having exchanged stares with this animal not once, but three times, something that is unlikely to occur except with a creature as poorly sighted as a deer. It is interesting, as well, to try to analyze any given encounter from the perspective of the wild animal, which will diverge least from the human perspective in the case of a creature that is relatively unafraid of man.

One June day in 1989, not long before dusk, I had been sitting quietly in front of my cabin for some time when I decided to take a towel off the line and tuck it away inside the cabin. As I returned toward the open door from inside, I heard the sound of a heavy animal fleeing into the woods to the southeast. There was not a single snort such as a deer would normally have made, nor the characteristic sound of hoofbeats. Since I was down wind from the animal and not making much noise, it seems probable it had come far enough up onto the outcrop to have seen me moving about, from a distance of thirty-five yards or so. It made me wonder whether I had possibly missed seeing a bear—or even a mountain lion—by my inopportune activity.

Between the Badlands and the northeastern end of the Crags is a lowland within which flows a small tributary of the Fly Brook. A large beaver pond and dam that I've often visited have provided a number of wildlife sightings for me, due to the presence of water and a lack of screening. Over the years I've seen here a great horned owl, a duck with its brood of ducklings, and a spotted fawn, as well as the pond's architects and builders themselves.

The beavers, having returned to this pond after a prolonged absence, stayed for three or four years and then abandoned it once again sometime in 1982 or '83. On a day hike in October of the latter year, I discovered that most of the water had drained out through some small holes in the dam's bottom, leaving hardly more than a large puddle where there'd been a pond over an acre in extent. The dam has not been repaired. After my initial dismay, I learned at least to enjoy the greater ease with which the beaver dam could now be crossed and to observe with increasing interest the gradual evolution of the former pond into a beautiful wetland meadow.

A few minutes east of the pond stood a dead pine tree about sixteen or eighteen feet in height that seemed to be a favorite roost of a trio of vultures. A friend and I once were able to approach within five or six yards before the last of these great birds lost its nerve and flew off; on a subsequent occasion, while alone, I stood atop the ledge at the tree's very base, my head no more than a dozen feet from the nearest of the birds, without precipitating their departure. This tree was a landmark along the footpath southwest of Mud Pond, and survived the fierce winds of the great March blizzard only to be felled ignominiously in the spring of '93, perhaps by some miserable soul offended at a thing manifesting greater character in death than that possessed by the saw-wielding vandal in life.

Turkey vultures may look huge, with their wingspans of

five or six feet, but they are nearly all feathers and in fact weigh only four or five pounds. This wing-to-weight ratio helps make them magnificent at soaring. The big birds they were named for weigh two or three times as much and are somewhat unwilling flyers, preferring to launch themselves downslope so as to become airborne without actually having to gain much altitude. The wild turkey has become well established here in the Shawangunks only in the past two decades, after an absence of well over a century. It prefers heavily wooded slopes, and I've never encountered one in the pine barrens. Once, as I zigzagged along among fallen tree trunks in the hardwoods south of Mud Pond, I made a sudden left turn around an obstacle and flushed a turkey I hadn't seen, from a distance of no more than eight feet.

I have at last count seen a total of eight rattlesnakes in the Shawangunk Mountains. One was actually down *inside* the most open and accessible of the Ellenville Ice Caves. I was hiking with a group of college students at the time, and as we approached the cave, some other hiker who was exiting told us of the rattler down near the bottom. We made our descent and found it sure enough, some fifty or seventy-five feet below the surface, nearly immobile from the cold. How it got there is difficult to guess: It seems unlikely that any right-minded snake would decide to stray into the depths of that cavern under its own power, considering the cool draft that emanates from below; as well it seems improbable that anyone had captured the snake and brought it into the hole; and whether a three and a half-foot snake could withstand a free fall from such a height uninjured also seems dubious, unless perhaps it had landed tail first, coiled like a spring!

At any rate, one of my companions immediately proposed constructing a proper contraption from a piece of cord and a stick: The snake's neck safely confined and its body supported with another stick, we carried the creature to the surface and released it into the bushes. When we looked in on it after the warmth had returned to its bones, we found it coiled with its head up and tongue darting in and out, obviously aware that something terrifying had transpired, but apparently none the worse for its adventure.

I encountered a rattler when picking huckleberries near Mud Pond in August of 1983, a little southwest of the lake's outlet. I had nearly filled my picking container and decided it was time to deposit its contents safely in my backpack, which stood twenty-five or thirty yards distant. My course led through knee-high crackerberry bushes, but along the way was a low ledge of rock, a natural stepping-stone. I was one step away from putting my foot onto that ledge when I arrested my stride in mid course, nearly throwing myself off balance. For on the rock a rattlesnake lay coiled.

At first I contemplated whether the snake could already have been alerted to my presence. But soon I realized that its coiled shape did not indicate a striking position; it was apparently just taking a late-morning snooze. I threw a little stick its way to get a rise out of the snake but got no reaction. I tossed a larger piece of wood, punky and dead, that I knew wouldn't hurt the creature, but still got no more response than a few flicks of its tongue. Before long I was standing nearly alongside the rattler, gently pinning its neck down with a dead forked stick I'd found. Although there is no question regarding the snake's identity, and though the temperature was in the 70s after a fairly mild night, the snake never shook its tail at me nor assumed a hostile position. It merely uncoiled itself and slowly made off toward the bushes, as if feeling nothing more serious than a mild annoyance at having its privacy disturbed.

How unlike was the disposition of the next rattlesnake I encountered! In June of 1993 I was hiking with a friend along the path from Sunrise Rock toward High Point; we were several minutes north of the lowest elevation along the trail, and had just passed the second little stream. No sooner did I set foot onto a small outcrop than a rattlesnake fifteen feet in front of me whipped its body instantaneously into a tight coil, its tail raised in a frenzy of buzzing.

After seeing two rattlers, each probably better than four feet in length, on consecutive days of a berrypicking trip in late August of 1995, I decided to invest in a pair of snake-proof gaiters.

Early one June morning in 1992, I arose and stepped outside my cabin briefly to take stock of the weather; leaving the door wide open, I returned to bed for a while, prior to getting dressed and washed. A quarter hour later, as I lay there on my back, gazing out at the view, a porcupine suddenly poked his nose inside the doorway and put one paw down on the cabin's floor, before I spoke up, chiding him for his rudeness; whereupon he backed out, turned around, and ambled down the length of the outcrop and into the woods.

Had Porky succeeded in taking up residence with me, he would not have been my only tenant. For it was just about a year prior to this that I discovered a creature already dwelling within the confines of my cabin. I was half-standing, half-leaning against the exterior south wall, when my attention was attracted by a barely audible disturbance among dead leaves near the cabin's southwest corner. Soon a fully grown snake emerged from the bush. Now I don't care how many times one has seen a milk snake—when those alternating bands of brown and tan appear suddenly in serpent form, there's a moment when one's blood runs cold. You can imagine my dismay when this fellow then proceeded to disappear into a little hole between the stones of the cabin's wall.

My first response was to ascertain that the interior mortar work formed a more effective seal than that of the cabin's exterior. Then I thought to plug up the hole after the snake had left the next morning. But it soon dawned on me that he was really causing me no harm nor inconvenience, and so before long I was planning how I'd use some pine needles in front of the opening to determine the snake's comings and goings so I could watch for him to make his appearance. This has now become something of a pastime on lazy June days, and a week or two at the cabin in this season would no longer seem complete without a few sightings of my mute companion.

Early one summer evening many years ago, a tiny ring-necked snake crawled through the open door of my cabin while I was up on the roof enjoying wind and mist. Since then, having in mind the reptilian diversity of my environs, I've always followed a precaution of keeping the door shut unless I'm present either within the cabin or just outside the door. Even in the latter instances, I like to give a glance over to the doorway every so often, just in case. While I was eating lunch inside the cabin one sultry day in June of '84, I gave the doorway just such a routine glance and was quite astonished to see another ring-necked snake that had obviously entered the cabin just moments before. There was a powerful sense of déjà vu as well as a reminder that my alertness had not been without justification.

A year later I was seated indoors, finishing up supper, occasionally looking up through the open door to note the gradually changing landscape: Shadows lengthened, and bands of clouds arrived and departed seemingly at random, as the June sun began its final hour or two of descent toward the horizon of pines behind me. It was then that I saw the bobcat.

I am certain no sound had attracted my attention, it was merely a casual glance out through the doorway that brought my eyes to a tawny creature that had passed right to left, twenty-five yards from my cabin door, and was now entering some bushes that form an irregular band of vegetation between sections of the outcrop. What I saw was that portion of the animal's body to the rear of its front legs: the side, hindquarters, and stubby tail—a creature somewhere in the range of about twenty-five to thirty-five pounds. Laughable though it may seem, the very first thought that crossed my mind for an instant was "cocker spaniel," my being reminded of the rather ill-tempered bobtailed bitch of about the same size and color that I'd often seen at a friend's house during childhood. The creature was out of sight in scarcely half a second, and I immediately realized what it was that I had seen.

I jumped to my feet and moved quickly and quietly down the outcrop toward the south, searching ahead and toward my left in hopes of getting a better look. The thought racing through my mind was of the utter inadequacy of this experience—of the prospect that the animal would hear my footsteps, flee, and I'd have to content myself with having viewed the rear end of this beast in a less than magnificent pose, so lacking in wild grandeur that I'd been able to imagine it for a moment as the yapping canine of childhood memory. I arrived nearly alongside of where the creature had been when I'd seen it, and suddenly there it was again, a hundred feet to the east, the length of its body perpendicular to my line of sight, standing or crouching somewhat with its head turned toward me. It was immediately apparent that it had heard my footsteps and had been *awaiting my appearance*, much as I had awaited the deer two years before. For about ten seconds, the bobcat and I stared directly at each other. It would have been both futile and dishonest to attempt to conceal either my presence or my awareness of its presence, so I moved my head about freely in order to compensate for a low pine branch halfway between us that partially blocked my view of its face.

I was able to make out clearly the texture of the region where the cat's whiskers emerged from the front of its face, also the ears, which seemed somewhat rounded, certainly not tufted like those of a lynx. What I viewed bore more resemblance to a small lion than to a house cat. It became increasingly obvious that this was not an encounter in which I was free to manipulate the reaction of the other party, that in fact I was being observed as much as doing the observing. I even began to wonder whose turn it was to make the next move.

I wish now that I had talked to it. But I was of course loath to do anything that might scare the creature away. Finally the wildcat responded to my greater size and apparent boldness by striding forward and onto some rocks—thus momentarily becoming fully visible—and then leaping off and disappearing into the forest, along a game trail that I often use myself. This was truly a beast of the wilderness, and I was under the distinct impression that it had never made eye contact with a human before, nor seen one except perhaps from a considerable distance.

After waiting nearly a quarter-century to see my first bobcat in the wilds, I saw my second one four months later, in the hardwoods halfway down the mountain slope toward Upper Mountain Road. Though it was not as exciting for me as my primal encounter, and there was no real interaction between us, the experience is nevertheless worth retelling. At the time I was with a friend who had joined me for two nights at the cabin, helping to carry some plate steel with which to reinforce the door. While at the cabin, I had entertained my guest and myself by re-enacting for him the wildcat sighting of the past June: We'd taken turns playing the bobcat, where it was when first I'd seen it and where it was standing when we'd seen each other, while my partner or I looked on from inside the cabin or from the outcrop. It is noteworthy that my companion, who hailed from the wilds of West Hartford, had never so much as seen a deer until accompanying me on this outing, when a young doe had unaccountably charged nearly toward us and across the footpath not six feet in front of me as we made our way up the trail on the lower slopes of the mountain.

Returning from the cabin, approaching the place where the old trail (now obliterated by logging operations) descended to a wet, level area close to the Beaver Brook or Dwaar Kill, I heard a large animal make a quick dash, about a hundred feet off to my right; through the trees I caught a blur of tan or brown moving from left to right, back uphill, just our side of the stream. The sound was too low to the ground to be a deer, with too much noise of dead leaves.

The movement stopped, but the animal was no longer in view. At that moment my friend, who was five or ten yards behind me, said, "bobcat!" As he later described it, he had not seen that first dash of the animal but now had a fairly clear view of it, standing with something black in its mouth, perhaps a bird. A moment later the cat came back downstream; my companion was now close behind me, and we both obtained a good view of a full-grown wildcat, front end crouching down with its prey, rear end raised toward us, with bobtail conspicuously visible. The creature then obliged us by turning clockwise somewhat, so that we got more of a profile and could briefly see its entire body and head, as it stood more erect. It had apparently released its game, as a tease, as so often I have seen domestic cats do. For there followed another quick spring, at an angle, to the right and away from us, across the stream, as the cat retrieved its prey before taking it up the steep embankment and out of sight. Apparently that first swift movement I saw was the initial spring and capture, taking the cat outside my view but into that of my companion. The animal appeared somewhat darker and larger than the one I saw in June, both undoubtedly due to the growth of a winter coat.

I saw my third bobcat on the thirteenth of June of '97, while I sat at the foot of the guest bed in my cabin, watching a light rain shower through the open doorway as a cold front passed over the mountain. It was close to nine P.M., and the cat seemed almost an apparition in the fading light, its coat lustrous from the rain as it crossed the outcrop, walking erect and confident in a graceful stride. It was headed northwestward and thus approaching me at an angle; I attempted a rendezvous on the open rocks to my right, after it disappeared behind a clump of vegetation just south of the cabin, but it had apparently become alert to my intentions and diverted toward the south-southwest. For it never emerged from behind the thicket, but vanished as silently as it had appeared.

During the latter part of the 1970s, reports began confirming the advent of coyotes to the Shawangunk region (and indeed much of the East), and a prediction was subsequently published that this animal might soon become the dominant mammalian predator of these mountains. About the winter of 1982/83, a friend told me of hearing a strange barking sound, as if made by several animals together, while he and some buddies were camping near the beaver pond. The sound, said he, while dog-like, was nevertheless distinct from any utterance that dogs could possibly take credit for.

It was in June of 1984 that I heard this sound while at my cabin. The first time it was somewhat muffled, coming from down wind (from the southeast), seemingly from a great distance, during mid morning. But the next day, about nine forty-five in the evening, I heard clearly and more loudly a sound that could be nothing else than coyotes, emanating from the north-northeast, about the direction and distance of the Red Spruce Swamp. Six days later I heard them again from the north, at half past four in the morning. On both of the latter occasions the cabin windows were open, with screens in place, and both times I was able to rush outside and listen to this strange, soprano yapping and yowling without even the impediment of the cabin's walls. During the evening occurrence I could detect, at the very end of the short serenade, one or two barks from a distinct individual, like the sound of a horn player finishing a lively tune a couple of sixteenth-notes behind the other members of his band.

I had hoped that, having apparently settled themselves into the most remote part of the Shawangunks, my coyote neighbors would become a permanent presence in the Badlands, and their eerie calls would be something I could look forward to hearing often. I was disappointed in that expectation, for it was not until a decade later that I began hearing them once again from my cabin. But since the late 1980s, their wailing has occasionally resounded through the woods and meadows around my home in the Wallkill Valley. Unintimidated by the presence of man, the majority of these creatures seem to have opted for a valley habitat, with its greater ecological diversity and abundance of game.

The mating of coyotes and domestic canines, producing the so-called "coy-dog," is believed by wildlife experts to be a short-lived expedient that occurs only when the coyote population is too sparse in a given region to permit adequate availability of mates. The offspring of such a union often do not do well, and the local coyote population has long since become large enough to obviate such cross-breeding. The larger size of the Eastern coyote, as compared to those familiar to folks in the Western states, is due not to cross-breeding with dogs, but rather, apparently, to improved diet, or to natural selection already at work, with breeding favoring longer-legged animals better suited to the greater range and larger prey typical of the Eastern coyote.

The wild, thrilling sound of these creatures is one that may in fact hark back to the time of the Indians and early settlers. For there is a current theory that the "wolf" reported by the seventeenth- and eighteenth-century colonists was perhaps not the timber wolf at all, but rather the same creature that is present today. (It is considered doubtful that wolves and coyotes would both have been present, for wolves would likely drive out their less powerful cousins.) The coyote of today might thus have simply returned to its old territories in much the same way as the mountain lion is apparently attempting to do.

CHAPTER 10

Atmosphere

When I take up residence on the mountaintop for a portion of June each year, it is in part for the opportunity to witness changes that accompany the seasonal transition from lingering cold to precocious heat. The atmosphere is often dynamic, as the jet stream wavers back and forth across the middle latitudes. One June I recorded the passage of eight distinct weather fronts in less than two weeks, and in 1988 the temperature went from 33° on the tenth of the month to 93° six days later. When I visit my cabin in mid winter, I have no interest in seeing mild, pleasant weather but am there to experience immersion in one end of the weather spectrum: I go up hoping for snow and an arctic cold wave and even feel dispirited if the weather proves insipid and uneventful. Over the years, the journal in which I write whenever I'm at my cabin has recorded a wide assortment of meteorological events from various seasons. These have determined my activities, influenced my moods, and provided me with both entertainment and inspiration.

The year that began my annual June camping trips was 1980. Having grown accustomed to camping in July, I neglected to appreciate that early June is not yet summertime in the Shawangunks. A cold front arrived on the afternoon of the eighth, when temperatures were sufficiently mild to permit me to lather up and shower under the cabin's roof gutter during the heavy downpour that accompanied the front's passage. My journal records the progress of the weather that followed:

The thermometer plunged all during the afternoon and at bedtime reads 40°. An hour ago I lit a fire in my potbelly stove. A pleasant treat to be able to cozy up around a fire in the month of June! The sky has now cleared and the stars are shining brilliantly.

Monday evening June 9—*I awoke shortly before sunrise to find the thermometer registering 32° plus a hair's-breadth. When I walked outside I tried rubbing a little rainwater from the pail onto the edge of the roof gutter but could not produce any frost. I made a fire and ate breakfast.*

Late in the morning, when the temperature had risen to the mid fifties, cloudiness set in from the northwest and we had some sprinkles—the usual instability following a cold front, I supposed. But after lunch, I stepped out to find a lowering ceiling and clouds coming from the west-southwest at a quick pace. The sky showed turbulence induced by the mountain.

The thermometer, which had been holding steady at 43° since the clouds set in before lunch, now began a steady rise to 50° as we apparently experienced another short-lived warm sector. There followed a slight but significant change in the sky and a wind shift to westerly, and though there were some more light showers, the humidity seemed to be dropping.

I rekindled a fire in the stove when I came indoors before noon and have kept it going all day long. This was almost like a winter day at the cabin, with many lazy hours spent tending the fire, heating up some hot chocolate, soup, etc. The temperature has been so greatly below normal that I must confess to being somewhat under-prepared in terms of clothing. I was essentially cabin-bound all afternoon, and though I occasionally stepped outdoors to look at the sky and get a few minutes of fresh air, I could not have stayed out for very long. I've been thinking about 1816, the "Year Without a Summer," and the eruption last month of Mount St. Helens!

On the tenth, with partial sunshine, the weather moderated slightly, but by bedtime the thermometer had slid back down to 39°. At dawn on June 11, I stepped outside to find the thermometer holding at precisely the freezing mark, though once again I was unsuccessful in producing frost.

Contemplating the possibility of cold and inclement weather on the day of my return trip to the valley (Friday the thirteenth!), I engaged in some contingency planning:

> I fashioned a get-up to provide head and neck warmth, utilizing one towel as a scarf, another wrapped over my head and around my ears and pinned under my chin. My faithful old felt hat would fit over this, with a chin strap of cotton twine fastened to the hat band on either side. On top would be a waterproof kerchief made from my scrap piece of coated nylon, tied under my chin and sewn or pinned to the front of my hat brim.
>
> I have only one pair of clean wool socks left, but I aired out a dirty pair to use as mittens. I put this all together temporarily and took a photographic self-portrait, holding the camera at arm's length. Quite a sight.

Rarely do I experience in fair weather the deep sense of

being ensconced in the mountain that I often feel when my cabin is socked in the clouds. Over the years this phenomenon has occurred, on the average, during at least a portion of one in every four days at the cabin. I won't go quite so far as to say that I consciously look forward to such weather, and after a day or two of fifty-yard visibility, I do yearn for dry air and bright sunshine again. But on occasion, just when I least expected it, I have awakened some morning to realize that my planned trip to the Red Spruce Brook is off for the day and that the mountain and sky have decided to take command; in such instances I am quite content to sit back and watch the drama unfold, though in truth I have not much to say in the matter.

Because of its lofty elevation, Castle Point is most often the first in clouds. But nearly as often, a lowering altostratus overcast will still be thousands of feet overhead (as confirmed by the apparent altitude of visible aircraft) when suddenly mist will start creeping over the front of the ridge near Mud Pond or into the spruce and hemlock glens farther east along the range. Then, to my south, dark, amorphous clouds come charging up over the far end of the Crags from the Verkeerder Kill gorge, racing low overhead, northeastward along the natural flyway formed by the topography. From my location I'm able to watch the progress of this river of mist as it overflows its banks and creeps higher up the slope toward my cabin.

At a certain point I can no longer see even the top of the Crags, and it is apparent the clouds have ascended the slab cliff onto the plateau of the Badlands. There is a moment of anticipation that becomes suspended in time, as the clouds progressively engulf terrain that is hidden from my view by the curve of the slope. I am on a small island, cut off from the world, as a wall of grayish white to my southeast intensifies as it approaches, like some enormous tidal wave. After perhaps five or ten minutes, treetops at my nearest horizon, two or three hundred yards off, suddenly reveal shrouds of blowing mist. Then nearer bastions fall in succession to the invading cloud mass, until finally, that first tongue of mist breaks into my own rock outcrop. Moments later, the cabin itself is engulfed. The temperature will hover about the low fifties and I'll pass this day in contemplation, savoring the companionship of the fire in my wood-burning stove and the simple pleasure of a pot of pork 'n' beans. Soon enough the weather will change; I'll be at my swimming hole once again, none the worse for a day or two spent peering into the wind, rain, and mist from my perch high in the pine barrens.

When I purchased my iron stove the year I completed the cabin, it came accompanied by instructions warning of the necessity for an adjustable barometric draft regulator in the stove pipe. I complied, and when replacing the stove pipe years later, I replaced the first draft regulator with a second one of more or less similar design. The function of this device is to prevent the fire from burning too hot at times when gusty winds increase the flow of air up the flue: At such moments the regulator is sucked open, admitting extra air into the flue at a point well above the firebox. When the draft door is drawn open by the wind, it bounces shut with a gentle clanging or banging noise that is not at all unpleasant. There are generally six to eight audible bounces, with often nearly half a second elapsing between the first and second one, each succeeding bounce coming at rapidly diminishing intervals. The volume of sound likewise diminishes with each bounce.

Anyway, although this device has never proven itself to be quite so essential as the original instructions made it appear, I have nevertheless grown accustomed to its characteristic sound during times of high wind. When the wind is blowing during stormy or threatening weather, I often use the draft regulator as a primitive anemometer of sorts. I set the adjustment so that the draft door will be sucked open every minute or two, at the highest wind gusts currently being experienced. Over a period of time, I can then tell by the volume of the draft regulator's sound and the frequency of occurrence whether the wind is rising or subsiding. The occasional soft clanging of the draft door within the cabin becomes an integral part of the storm's music, a gentle, almost plaintive echoing of the tempest without.

A storm I weathered at my cabin in June of 1982 combined wind, rain, and blowing mist and lasted three days in its various manifestations. The afternoon preceding the storm saw a developing overcast and a fresh southeast wind, backing to easterly by late in the day.

Saturday night June 5—Socked in all day, visibility ranging from something over a hundred yards down to fifty. A northeast wind gusted to 25 m.p.h., and precipitation varied from a fine drizzle to moderate rain. The day's temperature ranged between 51° and 56°.

After breakfast I spent some time outdoors enjoying the storm. Later in the morning I made a fire in the stove, shaved and washed up a bit, and lounged comfortably in a T-shirt and dry jeans while some of my garments hung on nails around the stove to dry.

About 6:30 the sky lifted somewhat and visibility improved to about a mile. Thereafter the ceiling alternately rose and fell. But rain and wind continue unabated.

Sunday evening June 6—For the first half of today, wind, mist, and precipitation were slightly less severe than yesterday. From mid afternoon on, however, it rained almost continuously, frequently with moderate force. The wind increased somewhat, gusting at times to about 30 m.p.h. and hurling the raindrops against the east wall with vehemence. Temperatures held between 54° and 56° most of the day. As yesterday, the ceiling occasionally lifted and fell.

I kept a small fire going from late in the morning nearly till bedtime, at first largely for its drying effect but later for its warmth, as the thermometer dropped to 50° and the wind intensified. There is hardly a dry place on the floor to set my feet on. Though this storm has put on a decent show at times, I am ready for sunny weather.

Monday night June 7—*A change in the weather at last:* By daybreak the sky had lifted off the mountain and by mid morning we were experiencing brief sunny spells. Visibility was generally fair, though mist hung over the Hudson River for parts of the day, obscuring the Highlands.

I removed firewood and various other items from the cabin, did a good sweeping and all-around housecleaning, and aired things out. In the afternoon I collected more wood and sawed it up. Found a deer carcass from this past winter a hundred yards to the southwest.

The storm was not ready to give up quite yet: Clouds persisted and eventually reformed themselves into an overcast. A fresh northeast wind continued and the temperature stayed below 60°. Around five o'clock Castle Point got socked in, and soon the clouds were upon us once more. But about 6:30 they lifted somewhat, and from then till bedtime the bottom of the cloud cover ranged back and forth between about 2000 and 2200 feet above sea level, while the wind gusted to 30 m.p.h.

I hiked out to the highest part of the cliff overlooking the upper Verkeerder Kill and followed north a ways. The clouds gave a spectacular performance—frequently

I was surrounded by swirls of billowing mist, yet could see clearly out through the bottom of the cloud layer and off the edge of the mountain range into the valley, even twenty or thirty miles distant. Tongues of mist invaded the pine barrens on all sides, whipped about by the wind, while barely above my head, amid occasional flashes of blue sky, the dark cloud masses rushed out over the brink of the cliff and across the rich greens of the Verkeerder Kill basin to collide head-on with the upper regions of the Sam's Point plateau. Off to the south and southwest the valley and distant hills were dark blue under the brooding sky.

I returned to the cabin, changed into dry clothes, and made supper. Castle Point remained in the clouds, but at my elevation we were sometimes in, sometimes out. For much of the time the front ridge was clearly visible under the overcast and the lights in the valley shone brightly, even when seen through a veil of blowing clouds. At bedtime the thermometer reads 47°.

The next morning, though the sky was still gray, the clouds were well above the mountaintop. The sun broke through in stages, getting rapidly bolder as the morning progressed. We were still under the influence of the storm until early afternoon, when the wind died down considerably, becoming somewhat more northerly, and clouds began to be scarce. Its theatrics over with after three days, the storm had finally dissipated to some faint mutterings near the eastern horizon.

While sunbathing outside the cabin's south wall during Indian summer weather in October 1981, I got an idea for constructing a removable solarium that could permit similar activity (or lack of activity) in wintertime. The next day I constructed a four-piece frame of red maple, and I subsequently brought to the cabin a nine- by twelve-foot polyethylene drop cloth to be fastened to this frame. I got to christen my invention a few months later during what turned out to be several of the coldest days I've ever experienced at the cabin. I arrived on January 10 and wrote the following:

> *I was pleasantly surprised to find a full foot of moderately soft snow on the mountain. In the valley there's only about four inches of hard, icy snow left from the three storms of mid December. I switched from crampons to snowshoes as soon as I left the footpath, near Mud Pond. We had some snow showers. The weather turned cold yesterday and intensely cold today: When I reached the cabin about 12:30 I found the thermometer at $-1°$, the high reading for the day.*

I opened up the cabin, made a trip to the Little Kill for water, watched the moon bounce its beams off Lake Awosting, and made a coal fire for the night. The wind was averaging about fifteen miles per hour, gusting to twenty-five, with some blowing snow. The bedtime temperature reading, $-8°$.

Monday night January 11—*This morning's thermometer stood at $-11°$. The chill factor was sustained at $-45°$ all night. Today's weather was mostly sunny, but with snow showers for much of the morning and again toward sunset. Visibility, which had been good yesterday, deteriorated to fair, except poor during the snow. The high temperature was $+7°$. Winds were a shade lighter than yesterday.*

After a breakfast of bacon and eggs, I spent a few hours sawing firewood from a large fallen birch tree in the woods to the southeast. I also freed up my coal pile and brought in tonight's supply to thaw out. Once the day's work was accomplished, I got the cabin nice and warm, changed into my jeans and cotton sweatshirt, ate a leisurely lunch, and spent the rest of the day relaxing. After holding at zero for several hours, the thermometer reads +1° at bedtime. It is snowing lightly again.

Tuesday night January 12—Last night's thermometer was deceiving, for the early morning temperature exactly tied yesterday's frigid reading. Just before daybreak I made a necessary trip to the outhouse, setting a personal record-cold as far as that particular activity is concerned. The moderate to fresh breeze continued during the coldest part of the morning (−45° chill factor) but became light during the mid-day period. Visibility was fair and a bright sun shone.
 I ate breakfast, sawed up some logs, and shaved. Then I went to work on my solarium. Shortly after noon, with the thermometer at +11°, I crawled inside and was soon basking nude. I not only kept cozy for three hours but also saved a heap of fuel by letting the fire burn out. Once inside the solarium, when I unfolded my foam pad for a beach chair, to my surprise out popped a cardboard hitchhiking sign that I'd forgotten was still in there. Appropriately enough, the sign proclaimed in large, red letters: MIAMI. On the reverse side, in blue, was the word NORTH. At bedtime the thermometer reads −3°.

Wednesday night January 13—The early morning temperature was +7°, the first indication of a change in the weather. Daybreak brought view of some high, thin clouds and a very light sprinkle of fine snowflakes. For a while the sun came out and the sky almost seemed to be clearing, but the flurries continued and then the *clouds gradually reasserted themselves. After breakfast I made a trip on snowshoes for more water and spent the rest of the morning sawing the birch trunk. These pieces I split up with my hatchet.*

Shortly before noon the snow increased to light-to-moderate. The temperature held between 10° and 12°, a range from which it was not to depart for over twelve hours. After a few hours lounging indoors, I took a walk around the perimeter of my rock patch late in the afternoon to enjoy the wintery scene. By then there were three inches of new snow.

The breeze was so light as to be detectable only from the slight angle of the falling snow. This was southwesterly early in the storm, but northeasterly during the afternoon. During the evening the wind increased enough to become audible. Seven inches accumulated before the snow ended the next morning.

Thursday night January 14—*The sky remained solidly overcast all day, but Castle Point was clearly visible and some shapes in the valley were vaguely discernible for a while. Morning temperature was 17° and the high, a balmy 25°. I let the fire go out after lunch and spent a few hours inspecting the nearby woods for standing deadwood, to have some on hand in case severe weather should detain me an extra day. I brought back a few loads, but it is almost all of rather poor quality.*

About mid afternoon the air began to thicken, until Mud Pond was the farthest place I could see. I was sure we'd soon be socked in. The temperature fell rather quickly to 15°, but then held there and crept back up two degrees. After dark, visibility improved again. Now, at 1:00 A.M., it appears a cold front is sweeping all this weather eastward. The sky is clearing, breeze rising, and the thermometer has slipped to 13°.

The morning of the fifteenth brought a moderate to fresh northwest wind and bright sunshine, with a reading of 8°. Before closing up and leaving for the valley, I calculated the mean temperature for my time at the cabin, using each day's high and low readings. The average came to +6°, which compared very respectably with three mid-winter trips of similar duration I'd taken, at much higher elevations, in the Catskills and in the Presidential Range of New Hampshire's White Mountains.

In February of 1983 I hiked up to the cabin alone during a raging snowstorm that brought a foot of fresh accumulation by the time the precipitation ended late in the afternoon. I parked at the house of a friend who lived at the foot of the mountain. He drove me as far as his car could go up the steep, snow-covered road, where he hailed an acquaintance of his who was out on a snowmobile, and I transferred thereto for the last part of the road, to the trail head. Above Mud Pond, northeast winds were sustained at thirty to thirty-five miles per hour.

I find it more interesting, however, and more fun, to watch a storm develop after I've already settled myself comfortably into the cabin. In 1985 I enjoyed a winter storm that put on a respectable performance despite rather mild temperatures. I'd arrived with a friend on Saturday February 9, after a five-hour trip on snowshoes. There were areas of snow packed hard by the wind; elsewhere the ground cover was powdery, and it averaged just under a foot in depth. I had some problems with a new snowshoe harness I'd made, for the leather strap began to stretch and loosen. Carving steps in the windpack during steep climbs and traverses in the hardwoods just south of Mud Pond contributed to our slow pace. Above the lake, winds gusted to near fifty miles per hour. The temperature when we arrived at the cabin was 15°, at bedtime 10°, with the wind still blowing.

My companion was due home on Monday and hiked out alone. The day he departed began sunny and calm. My journal records the changes that ensued:

> *The sun was occasionally diminished by high, thin clouds. Temperatures ranged to a balmy 40°, the warmest reading I can recall in about a month. Visibility was poor to fair.*
>
> *During the evening a fresh southwest wind arose and medium-altitude cloudiness overspread the sky. The temperature held steady at 27°. By taking naps of a couple of hours' duration, with one lantern lit, turned very low, I am able to keep a wood fire going through much of the night. Awoke at 2:30 A.M. for the last time before finally retiring to sleep and found that we are socked in thick clouds, blowing from the south-southwest up to 20 m.p.h.*

Tuesday evening February 12—*By morning the wind had shifted to southeasterly, visibility at seventy-five yards. A thick rime coated the pine needles. About nine o'clock the first bit of precipitation began to fall, with the thermometer holding in the upper twenties. The wind had backed around farther, to the northeast by now.*

I set out with the aim of trying my hand at building a snow cave in a huge mass of windpack I'd noticed Saturday, drifted up against a ledge, just before the falls in the Little Kill. Using a carpenter's saw I brought from the cabin, and a snowshoe for a shovel, I made an entrance perpendicular to the drift and then turned sharp right and dug a seven-foot tunnel. I crawled in head-first, smoothed the arched ceiling, and contemplated returning after dark to spend the night there. My cave was limited by the width of the snow drift, so getting in and out of a sleeping bag would be quite a snowy affair.

By the time I returned to the cabin about 12:30, mixed snow, sleet, and (mainly) freezing rain had increased, and the wind had intensified. I was surprised to discover that the slight drop in elevation had brought me below the cloud layer as I approached the cabin — the valley was even faintly visible at first. But at this exposed location the northeast wind was considerably stronger than higher up by my snow cave.

During the next several hours the wind raged unceasingly, averaging about 25 m.p.h. but frequently gusting to 40 and 45, this at a height of only five feet or so above bedrock. Rain lashed furiously against the cabin's east wall. The barometric draft regulator on the stove pipe responded in kind with a continual din, while the door shook and the deer vertebrae strung on a cord outside rattled noisily against the south wall.

For half an hour it snowed heavily in big, wet, windblown flakes that careened promiscuously through the air, pelting the east windows like fast-moving miniature snowballs. Then the rain returned.

Once during late afternoon there was a heavy bombardment of ice pellets driven by a west wind; I felt sure this signified a cold front, but in a matter of minutes the wind had mysteriously backed around to the southeast. Visibility ranged mostly from sixty yards to about a mile, and the thermometer held just above freezing, rising briefly to 37° during the evening.

Because of the dampness, I had second thoughts about sleeping in my snow cave and opted for passing the night indoors instead. The next morning saw the mountain socked in again, with light snow falling, a temperature of 25°, and a moderate southerly wind. The wind veered to westerly during the afternoon, bringing colder temperatures and an end to the storm.

From the time of the cabin's construction—in fact from its very conception—I have wanted to be on the mountaintop to experience a first-class blizzard. But despite the considerable drama of the winter storm just described, a "respectable performance" does not a blizzard make. Through the early 1980s, when a couple of heavy snowstorms visited the Shawangunk region nearly every winter season, it seemed just a matter of time before my annual winter camping would coincide with one of these events. But then the snow stopped falling.

Seven, eight, nine winters came and went with only one major snow (January 1987) to break the pattern. My original skepticism that this could represent anything more than a temporary climatic wrinkle gradually gave way to the unavoidable impression that something basic had changed. Although it seemed likely that it might someday change back, there no longer seemed any certainty that this would happen anytime soon—or even in my lifetime, for that matter. And over the long run, the Greenhouse Effect was likely to hold sway.

Then came the winter of '92/'93 to proclaim that reports of Wintertime's demise had been greatly exaggerated! Early in the season there were several mostly wet, sloppy snows of moderate depth, nearly all ending with changeovers to freezing rain. "I suppose this passes for wintry weather nowadays," I wrote in a letter to my sister, mid-January. But most of these snows accumulated much more heavily in the Shawangunks than in the neighboring valleys. On February 12, a day after I'd come *down* from my cabin, a pattern began that established a continuous snow cover of five to ten inches in the valley and a gradually deepening snow pack at the higher elevations. Four weeks later, when weather forecasts warned of a mammoth winter cyclone of near hurricane intensity, I decided I could not miss this once-in-a-lifetime opportunity. On Friday morning March 12, I hurriedly readied my backpack, including, along with my usual winter gear, the barometer that hangs on my kitchen wall. I hiked up alone on snowshoes.

Arrived shortly after noon in beautiful, sunny weather. After poking around in the woods, I determined average snow depth to be about twenty-one and one-half inches—three times the depth in the Wallkill Valley. (On the south-sloping outcrop, sun and wind had reduced this figure by nearly half.) Before removing my snowshoes, I trampled a pathway to the outhouse, taking along my ash shovel to dig out the snow. I dug my woodpile free and took an extra firewood supply indoors.

Cirrus and cirro-stratus began creeping into the southern and southwestern sky during the course of the day and by dusk had formed a high overcast. At bedtime the thermometer read 16°. The barometer, adjusted to sea level, had actually risen a bit, to 30.30 inches of mercury. The air was perfectly still. It was the anniversary of that legendary storm of a century past that had become a reference point for all nor'easters, seemingly for all time to come.

My journal describes the storm's beginning:

> *During the night a fresh east wind arose, rattling one of the windows on that side of the cabin. After a while it subsided, no longer audible. The snow began falling shortly before dawn, thermometer at 17°, a reading from which it varied no more than a degree in either direction over the next eighteen hours. The barometer*

had begun its fall. After breakfast I went outside for more firewood. Snow was accumulating at a moderate to heavy rate, and the wind east-northeasterly, gentle to moderate.

By 10:20 A.M. the barometer had slipped to an even 30.00 and the wind, more northeasterly, was averaging 20 m.p.h.

I went outside before lunch to take in more wood and chop the very bottom row of large, unsplit logs off the bedrock. These I piled in the snow-free zone next to the east wall, formed by the cabin's deflecting the wind. Also used a snowshoe to shovel out the west window, which drifting snow had nearly blocked.

By this time (shortly before noon), new accumulation had reached several inches on the exposed outcrop and the wind was gusting to 40 and 45 m.p.h. in the highest treetops. Came inside and made a pot of soup, thickened with macaroni. The barometer was falling at the rate of .10 inches per hour.

I remained indoors for three and one-half hours. After lunch, I lay down awhile. Having spent much of the morning peering out the windows to gauge the storm's early development, I decided I could give it a rest and let the weather progress without my help. I knew I'd be going outdoors again eventually, for various necessary tasks and to experience the storm after it had had a chance to intensify. Expecting the wind to reach maximum force after nightfall, I wanted to save my excursion till late in the day. I planned to put on snowshoes and have a walk to the far end of the big outcrop a couple of hundred yards to the northwest. Meanwhile, as I lay on my bed, I could hear the sound of icy crusts sliding headlong across the cabin's roof, the old snow and ice broken loose by the rising wind. I had a smoke, and then, about a quarter past three, I cleared the condensation from my south window and took a good look outside for the first time in two hours.

Everything had changed in that space of time. Earlier the wind had been somewhat fitful, gusting unevenly, as if testing its powers and then pulling back for a moment's reflection before daring to assert itself once again. Now it seemed as though some critical stage had been reached: Like a swelling puddle of water that suddenly bursts its skin of surface tension to establish channels of outflow, the rising wind seemed to have breached an aerodynamic cushion formed by the intermittent vegetation and was now raging unchecked across the outcrop. The differential between sustained wind speeds and maximum gusts had narrowed, as had the difference between wind speeds close to the ground and in the higher treetops.

The storm had become a powerful machine, pumping a steady, unwavering deluge of blowing snow across my front yard at fifty miles per hour. Gusts reached perhaps sixty in the tallest trees beyond the edge of the outcrop. I had seen winter storms of such ferocity thirty years before, when, as a teenager, I'd played in bands entertaining American troops at Thule, Greenland, seven hundred miles north of the Arctic Circle. I had seen nothing like it since.

I checked the barometer. It had fallen .40 in two hours and stood momentarily at 29.20 inches. The storm center was not expected to pass at its closest till after midnight. *Could it be that the barometer would continue to plunge, and the wind to intensify, for yet another ten hours?* The prospect began to seem frightening.

As it turns out, there was little cause for alarm, for the dynamics of this storm were fundamentally different from those of a true hurricane. The wind had reached nearly a plateau, and did not increase markedly after this point.

When I prepared to exit the cabin shortly after 3:30, I carefully went over in my mind the most efficient procedure for accomplishing my several outdoor tasks with a minimum of fumbling. First among these tasks was to attach the window shutter to the smaller of the cabin's east windows, to stop a tiny but seemingly unpluggable current of wind and snow that shortly before had begun invading the cabin. After shoveling ashes from the bottom of the stove into the half-full waste-water bucket, I placed the latter on the floor near the doorway. Also placed within reach of the door my largest firewood basket, now empty, and a single snowshoe. I dressed for outdoors. The wind-chill was −28°, cold but not unusually so, and though I wore a wool pullover cap, I kept the hood of my parka down for greater visibility. I tucked the window shutter under my left arm, unlatched the door, and stepped out.

The wind and snow howling about my face were nearly overwhelming. Closing the door behind me, I found I could not attach the exterior hook and eye because heat from the door's crack had caused a mat of soft ice to build up on the sheetmetal of the door, where the hook's shaft must cross. With my hand I tried to jam the end of the hook into the eye, but then decided it would be a better idea to clear the ice away by fetching a screwdriver from inside the cabin. Had a brief fantasy of being stuck outside, unable to *re*open a frozen door! Did the job and left the screwdriver outside by the door, securely wedged. It was necessary to hitch the hook and eye each time I left the cabin, even momentarily.

I fastened the shutter over the window and retrieved the melt-water bucket, which I'd securely nestled into a hole chopped in the snow under the roof gutter the day before, when a brief period of dripping had ensued. Emptied the bucket of snow and placed it on the floor inside the door. Took out the waste-water bucket and dumped it outdoors at the usual place, being careful to stand up wind. I returned it to the cabin and grabbed my firewood basket. This I filled with the last remains of seasoned fuel. Had to chop some remaining ice off these logs. Returned the basket to the cabin and withdrew again, with the snowshoe. I circled around through the narrow snow-free corridor on the windward side and used the snowshoe to shovel out the west window. Returned to the cabin and took a breather for a minute.

Gaining confidence, I began the first of two recreational excursions around the outcrop, having tested the snow depth and found I could yet make my way safely. I'd long since given up the idea of trying to put on snowshoes and walking as far as the northwest outcrop.

I took frequent notes on the storm's progress which I transcribed to my journal the next day:

4:25 — A crash of thunder. One or two more, all moderate, but that was all.
4:30 — The barometer has slowed its fall. It reads 29.14.
4:50 — Went outdoors again, just for fun. The barometer had begun dropping vigorously again. Walked around the outcrop (with my hood on this time) and visited my three oldest trees. Watched from a distance as a gust of about 60 m.p.h. swept over the cabin, 70 m.p.h. in the treetops. But then the wind seemed to calm down somewhat, by the time I came back inside about 5:25.

The snow is only moderately dry and there's very little windpack occuring. Outside near the door, the dripping of water from the stove pipe and the shelter and heat from the cabin have created a small zone of wet, good-packing snow which I had to shovel away from the door. Dug out the west window again before coming in. It drifts half-over in half an hour.
6:15 — Barometer at 29.01. Winds have edged back up,

50 m.p.h. sustained across the outcrop, gusts to 60 or 65 in the treetops.

6:25 — The sound of water dripping onto the hot stove: Proved to be from melting snow flakes, the water having made its way along the horizontal length of pipe to exit from the elbow joint. This was the first time this has ever occurred. Attached a small waste pot to the stove pipe to catch the drip. It stopped when I went outside and removed all the ice build-up from the bonnet and the underside of the exterior pipe elbow.

6:35 — The barometer has free-fallen to 28.90.

7:00 — The barometer reads 28.88. The wind has increased to perhaps its strongest so far, based on the sound. By 7:20 the west window was completely obscured by snow again.

7:35 — After a pause, the barometer has resumed falling rapidly, to 28.83. While I stood with my nose out the door, there was a steady wind of about 65 m.p.h. sustained for what seemed close to a minute, right against the cabin's wall and in front of me across the outcrop. Must have been 75 or 80 m.p.h. in the treetops, though I couldn't see that far in the dark.

8:15 — The barometer at 28.82. By 8:25 it had plunged to 28.72, a rate of .60 per hour!

8:30 — The barometer reached 28.71, then rose a few hundredths before very gradually slipping again.

9:55 — I just returned from five or ten minutes outdoors. Cleared the west window again. Temperature still 17°. The snow and wind seem a little less intense now.

Shortly before midnight, having made a coal fire in the stove, I retired to bed. The storm had subsided greatly, sustained winds having fallen below gale force, though the barometer's continued fall had brought it to 28.63. At

1:50 A.M. I awoke for a moment and saw by my flashlight that it had dropped to 28.60. By 4:30 it was on its way up.

The storm has imprinted on my memory one visual image that stands out among the rest. It occurred when I had first dared to venture twenty-five or thirty yards down the outcrop. I turned around and stood there in the wind, looking back at the cabin. The gale raged before me in a constant flow, and I watched the cabin take a direct hit of about sixty miles per hour as a momentary concentration of blowing snow actually hovered for a tiny instant, caught by the wall and the roof's slight overhang, before venting furiously around this impediment and pluming out across the roof and into the treetops at near hurricane speed. I watched and I said to myself, nearly out loud, "This is how the cabin was always meant to look!" I was seeing something I'd always wanted to see, another of life's dreams that had finally been experienced as reality.

I returned, nearly against the wind, my hood still down, and decided I would be Charlie Chaplin, straining to re-enter his snowbound cabin in *The Gold Rush*, or maybe just some stranger who had unaccountably wandered into the Shawangunk Badlands to fight his way through the wind toward the haven promised by that small, symmetrical gray shape. I reached the cabin door, not without some difficulty, and was safely inside once again.

CHAPTER 11

Exosphere

FRIGID WEATHER has appealed to me ever since childhood, in part because it symbolizes the periodic reassertion of Nature's predominance despite repeated abuses heaped upon her by man. This is a role she can play as well in summer, when an angry thunderstorm can seem an act of defiance and redress or a victory shout to the banishment of foul, coastal, urban air by a cool, dry blast from the continental hinterland. One sultry day in June of '88, however, I had occasion to call into question my cold-weather bias: It was a day when the thermometer outside my cabin window soared to 93°. Humidity was such that the valley floor was only faintly visible, though mercifully, a moderate breeze held forth throughout the day. I had spent an hour indoors, where along with the shade, the coolness of the stone walls and floor offered some measure of relief. I smoked my pipe and then ate lunch, both of which had an additional, temporary cooling effect on my skin. Suddenly it dawned on me that I'd actually succeeded in becoming a trifle chilly. I stepped outside and felt the torrid blast as something momentarily welcome and even exciting: Was not this intense heat a natural phenomenon to be experienced for its own sake? Was not this an expression of Nature's dynamism? Carrying my foam pad to the rooftop, I surveyed the wilds in their veil of haze, then removed what little clothing

I'd had on and stretched out full length in the rays of the sun. I actually enjoyed this steamy sunbath for twenty minutes before once again seeking shelter indoors.

On hot, sunny days, if the prevailing wind is calm or nearly so, the mountain often creates its own breezes in the form of solar thermal currents. These arise on the southeastern face of the mountain, which lies at a slope and angle propitious for absorbing heat from the mid-morning sun. My cabin has a southeastern exposure but is set back at some distance from the cliff top; the movement of air may be barely enough to flutter the leaves of deciduous trees or these thermal breezes may approach moderate force and offer considerable respite from the sultriness of the day. Sometimes I've witnessed a congested cumulus cloud advancing toward me on gentle, westerly zephyrs aloft, only to be blocked in its forward motion by the opposing thermal currents, which thus denied me the comfort of the cloud's shade. At other times a long, straight row of small, white cumulus clouds will extend like a string of pearls above the southeastern escarpment, of a morning when the remainder of the sky is virtually cloud-free.

When the weather has been uncomfortably hot, there is no denying the drama and relief offered by a powerful thunderstorm. I've enjoyed a few good ones from my cabin's vantage point in the Shawangunks. One occurred in June 1984, following a week that saw the thermometer hit 90° on six of seven consecutive days, including 94° on the tenth of the month, the hottest day I've ever experienced at the cabin. It was also a week in which pitch pine pollen was thick in the air, forming a yellow haze in the wind. My journal entry of June 13 describes the storm that broke the heat wave:

> *The clouds built up to the north and a thunderstorm drifted lazily eastward over the mountain, with most of the lightning striking east and northeast of Lake*

Awosting. There was impressive vertical development in the clouds, though no cirrus top, and no precipitation visible underneath.

A while later thunder and more dark clouds began developing from areas directly to the west of here, and soon I was virtually surrounded by the storm. Lightning strikes were generally one to two miles distant. A good, solid downpour ensued. The first few gallons of water off the roof gutter looked like muddy outflow from a freshly-dug ditch, as a week's worth of pitch pine pollen washed off the roof. For a while I fancied perhaps the rain was yellow with pollen, but the water eventually cleared. I showered outdoors, first under the sky itself and then the rain gutter, and I brought the table and one floor mat outdoors for their own baths.

In an hour's time the temperature dropped from 92° to 62°, before rising back to 67°. The sky remained overcast, with a moderately high ceiling. So far there was no evidence of any frontal system, and even after the rain stopped the thick haze persisted. But about 7:30, a fresh display of low, dark clouds advanced purposefully from the northwest, the wind rose, and it was evident that the decisive moment had arrived. The front passed with a little more rain, though little of the earlier drama. Visibility improved markedly just after sunset, and the valley turned a beautiful dark blue-gray, fringed in places with mist. Castle Point had a brief encounter with a stray cloud.

The most intense electrical storm I've witnessed at the cabin occurred on June 15, 1986. It was not a frontal storm but rather was spawned over the Shawangunk ridge in unstable air and fed by updrafts that the mountain itself helped to generate.

With an early morning temperature already in the upper fifties, considerable cloudiness receding toward the east, and haze filling the valley, it was evident that a warm front had just passed through. The thermometer in fact reached 87° during the afternoon, and visibility continued poor during the entire day. A gentle to moderate westerly breeze kept things bearable, and I spent the warmest hours reclining lazily at various small shady spots around the outcrop.

By mid afternoon an imposing line of dark, fuzzy, congested cumulus clouds had formed parallel to the front of the ridge, as far as the eye could see in either direction, from Sam's Point to Minnewaska and beyond. Thunder rumbled with increasing frequency. About four o'clock the storm intensified over Sam's Point and started to move northeastward (and thus at a slight angle to the prevailing wind), directly toward this location.

The intense forked lightning and thunder seemed to rule out a much-desired shower under the roof gutter. As the storm descended, I sat on the guest bed and drew my feet up under me, making sure no part of my body was in contact with the stone. But just as the sky unleashed a heavy barrage of enormous raindrops and small hailstones, driven by a twenty mile per hour southwest wind, the lightning moderated. So I ran outdoors and lathered up. For a brief time, hailstones the diameter of mothballs fell, but upon examination they proved to be flattish pieces of ice with concave and convex sides—evidently, fragments of large hailstones that had broken apart while still airborne. The sun, low in the western sky, reasserted itself even as the precipitation was still falling. As the storm headed out over the upper reaches of the Peters Kill, a rainbow arched over the lowland nearby to my east, with the bow's apex over Murray Hill and the ends visible amongst individually distinguishable trees less than half a mile from my location. The sunlit cliffs of Castle Point were seen through the rainbow's translucent, multicolored light.

The most beautiful of sunsets on the mountain commonly occur on the heels of cold fronts, as the western sky clears and humidity drops, while clouds receding eastward reflect the setting sun's rays. The most exceptional sunset I've ever witnessed anywhere occurred June 10, 1981. I shared it with a young friend who had hiked in alone that afternoon to join me for two nights at the cabin. Toward evening, a few patches of blue sky began to appear through holes in an overcast. We were sitting in the cabin, talking, when I suddenly caught sight, through the window, of the orange glow of the setting sun reflected on Castle Point. I interrupted my own words mid-sentence and we headed out to take a look.

As soon as I stepped out the door, my companion right behind me, I did a double-take. What I had failed to see through the window was a fine, bright rainbow hitting the mountain just north of Castle Point. It arched around through the sky and plunged into the valley behind the Crags. At first only the ends were apparent, but steadily their arcs lengthened until the entire bow was visible. A definitive cold front had obviously passed through, and the wind aloft was due north. Midway between the two ends of the rainbow, hovering just leeward of the mountain, in line with the left end of the gap in the front ridge near Mud Pond, was a ragged, towering cumulonimbus cloud. It combined a dark, ominous-gray bottom with an intense orange-gold reflection above. Directly underneath, rain showers were falling into the valley, and this opaque haze was permeated with the same hues. To the imagination it appeared as though some powerful energy were radiating *up* from the valley and illuminating the cloud from within, the rainbow forming the outward wave front of this phenomenal event. Cradled beneath the huge arch, the mountain was aglow with its own characteristic response to the setting sun, the line between light and dark creeping upward from just below the level of the gap.

When a June day on the mountain opens with uncomfortable heat and humidity, I long for the arrival of a cold front and welcome even the temporary relief of a local thundershower. But these, of course, are only possibilities, and so I try to content myself with the weather at hand. I am loath to spend more than half of such days at my swimming hole, especially if the upper fall is not running or if the sky seems unsettled. Sometimes I have work to perform in connection with my firewood supply or the cabin's physical maintenance, at other times I may have writing or a hike in mind. But often as not, I'll choose simply to confront the specter of boredom by acknowledging that there's nothing at all to do besides preparing my meals and tending to the minor routines of daily life. Sometimes these days are most productive of all. For the eyes, ears, and mind wander about, seeking stimulus from the microcosm and discovering much that is fascinating from familiar places and things.

The imperative of keeping cool is often accomplished by following the diminutive tree shadows around the outcrop, taking advantage when shade is cast usefully onto open places, where it's comfortable to sit, and moving on when shadows dissolve into the bushes. This shadow-hopping has given me a degree of intimacy with the nooks and crannies of my front yard that I might not otherwise have attained. Once, while wandering about the outcrop, I swatted a fly that had alighted on my body, and I amused myself for over half an hour by watching an ant drag the carcass across the rocks. I was curious to discover the entrance to his nest and to learn the extent of his range. The ant carried his cargo for a distance of about twenty-five feet over diverse terrain, before describing a circle two or three feet in diameter, as he evidently lost his way. But no sooner did he complete the circle and begin his second go-round, than he realized his own confusion and abandoned his catch; after that it was impossible to follow him for long, for he now appeared like any ordinary ant, and besides, my eyes had grown as tired as his feet undoubtedly had.

A day such as one of these has hardly ever passed without my paying a visit to the three oldest pitch pine trees of my outcrop, located twenty to twenty-five yards in a southeasterly direction from my cabin. Core samples of these were taken at my suggestion by a Mohonk Preserve naturalist who visited me one June day in 1982. By far the largest and most vigorous of the pines, about six inches in diameter and fourteen feet high, is my chief shade tree on the outcrop. It revealed ninety-five growth rings. After allowing for two rings near the center that the coring tool missed and adding ten years for the tree to attain the two-foot height at which the core was drilled, the tree's year of birth may be estimated as 1875.

The middle tree, smallest of the three and in a state of decline, has a diameter of about five inches and a height of ten feet. It proved to be somewhat younger than the first, with an estimated origin about the year of the great blizzard.

The southernmost of the three I had guessed to be the oldest, for some younger trunks in the same soil mat appeared to be root suckers that had absorbed most of the new growth during recent decades. My companion concurred in this theory, and his coring tool revealed 103 growth rings. I call this the Grandpa Tree, for after making allowance for one missed ring and adding five years for the tree to reach the coring height of one foot, I deduced a year of birth about 1873, the year my maternal grandfather was born. Like the Blizzard Tree, Grandpa was already well into decline. In 1989 I noted one new pine cone, conceived from a flower of the previous spring. These were the final signs of reproductive vitality.

The tree's last, scant greenery turned to brown late in the summer of '92, and the following spring a friend and I made a tombstone, to record the years of birth and death. Sometime during the late autumn or winter of 1995-96, the tree was felled by a southeasterly gale. It reclines on the bare rock in full sun, its form and texture continuing to evolve in the characteristic manner; even in death, it is likely to beautify my front yard for years and perhaps decades to come.

Not far to the rear of the Grandpa Tree, another pine had already begun to achieve an aura of noticeable age and stature relative to its neighbors on the outcrop. It is the next generation, awaiting its turn: When Grandpa and the Blizzard Tree are dust, it will occupy a comparable position of prominence, second only to my shade tree, which, barring calamity, is likely to outlive us all.

In the forest several minutes from my cabin, a much larger pitch pine tree about thirty feet in height was the victim of a nor'easter sometime about 1983/84. The tree snapped at a point a few feet above the ground, but the trunk, though broken, was not severed. The foliage of the tree's crown lived on for another year or two before giving up the ghost. In June of 1987, I examined the tree with an eye to utilizing it for firewood. The trunk lay horizontal but elevated from the ground, supported by its base at one end and its crown at the other. Using my hatchet, I found it an easy matter to remove the bark, which sloughed off in large sheets, exposing thousands of tiny ants and a few slugs. The wood was thus better exposed to the air and a bit of sunlight, for proper seasoning. The trunk measured ten to twelve inches in diameter. I harvested a few nicely cured stumps of long-dead side branches, then returned with my saw and cut enough of the crown branches for two more loads in my backpack.

The next year, a camping companion and I began harvesting the fallen tree in earnest. Using a piece of old climbing rope I'd brought up the previous fall, I secured the trunk to a crotch eight or ten feet high in a sassafras tree standing alongside the pine. Then we cut off the crown, so that the trunk's weight was borne by the rope. We took turns cutting half a dozen fat pieces of firewood out of the log. I was disappointed to discover that the heartwood suffered from some rot, which seemed to get worse toward the base. I concluded the rot may more likely have been the cause, than the result, of the tree's demise.

This tree helped warm my cabin during three winter camping trips. When I made the last cut, I counted 115 to 120 growth rings. Toward the outer edge, the rings were so narrow as to be nearly indistinct, especially with the wood being somewhat punky. Adding ten years for the pine to reach the height of the saw cut (about six feet off the ground) brought the tree back to about 1855 or '60.

In 1989 I discovered a solitary young hemlock tree 200 or 250 yards from my cabin, in the woods near the edge of a sizeable rock outcrop. This tree was three feet in height when first I saw it, with a trunk as thick as my finger. It is noteworthy because there isn't another hemlock within about four-tenths of a mile, unless I be mistaken.

Immediately in front of the cabin door, there's a rock that I often use as a seat and a tiny clump of low-bush blueberries. The latter are among the earliest to ripen of any on my outcrop, apparently in a hurry to be eaten as quickly as possible. Adjacent to my seat is a patch of soil, perhaps the size of a bathtub, whose vegetation I've been keeping track of for over a decade. I was particularly interested in the progress of a few tiny pine trees that were trying valiantly to establish a footing here. Only one of these has survived: Born about 1985, it spent a few years adding annual segments of an inch or two before devolving to a two-segmented existence, with the second length of stem no more than a needle cluster and all the permanent growth concentrated in the original segment rising an inch and a half off the ground. The abundant rains of the 1990 season brought a renewal of growth, and by the spring of '94 a first pine cone had begun to form. By then the original trunk had attained a diameter of over an inch, with much slimmer woody stems extending out as far as an additional fourteen inches.

Not far below my door is a place where I dump the contents of my bucket of waste water from under the cabin's sink. The wood ash that I shovel into this bucket just before emptying it had sweetened the soil of this spot for upwards of twenty years when suddenly a lone dandelion appeared here. Whether a seed had hitched a ride with me or one of my guests, or whether it had traveled through the air from afar to this tiny island of alkalinity, I can not say; but there is now a thriving little colony of the plants. The dandelions' presence soon gave me the idea to plant some scallions and leaf lettuce here whenever I'm up to the cabin late enough in the winter or early enough in spring. I protect these under my wire firewood basket and enjoy them, with a few of the dandelion greens, during my June visit.

The bits of food crumbs that land here from my bucket have often attracted guests of the small, feathered variety. Typically, a single bird will be a frequent visitor for the duration of a particular camping trip. Once a black-capped chickadee who'd been cruising the spot alighted on some of my firewood, no more than an arm's length from where I was seated, and another year I spied a small, gray bird hopping about immediately in front of my door, gathering up a few strands of hair I'd removed from my comb, to line its nest. One afternoon, while two friends sat with me in the cabin, a bird who'd become nearly a constant companion flew in through the open door, about two or three feet above the floor, then recognized its error and flew back out again. A year later, this individual or another of the same species entered my cabin briefly while I was busy with breakfast; before making its departure, it alighted on an unoccupied wire clothes hanger that hung suspended from a nail, causing it to swing daintily like a canary's perch in a cage.

Sometimes in June, if I feel the notion to go on a small hike, or when some practical consideration takes me in that direction, I pay a visit to the Bog, lying just above the Lost River. Lingering near its edge for half an hour or so, I let my eyes peruse this physiographic anomaly, while the song of the hermit thrush may float to my ears, mingling with the ethereal cadences of the myrtle warbler. My thoughts wander back to that first summer, when I was a frequent visitor here, my feet leaving a wake through the sea of leather-leaf as I carried supplies and materials to the site of the cabin. There is a shrub of mountain laurel on the northwest shore bearing flowers rich in pink; if the season is right, I gather some cuttings for my vase, and the cabin is beautified for days by the delicate blossoms—a luxury and indulgence I could scarcely have imagined, that June so many years ago.

Over the decades, there are experiences that stand out in my memory not so much for their drama as for their being so entirely unexpected. The following entry describes a day visit I made to the cabin with a friend, October 22, 1979:

> *During the afternoon we stood on the roof, enjoying the colors and textures as sunlight and shadow passed alternately over the mountain. The barely perceptible southerly breeze brought occasional leaves fluttering down through the air. We soon became aware that these were coming into view at elevations significantly higher than the treetops! Like snow flakes from a clear sky in advance of a squall, the gently twirling travelers had no apparent source, and their visitation at that calm and virtually silent hour filled the mountain with an almost mystical presence. We began speaking in whispers. Scanning the air, we watched for them as one might look for meteors on a starlit night—their golden forms, descending in slow motion from the open sky, seemed to arrive from origins no less intangible.*
>
> *After several minutes the mystery was solved when*

a fresh southerly wind met our faces, apparently trailing behind the unencumbered air of higher elevations. The leaves had been swept from the southeast slope of the mountain, carried in updrafts over the Crags, and had journeyed over half a mile northward before falling into calm air nearer the ground and being freed from captivity to sail gently into view.

On a recent June camping trip, I was puttering around inside the cabin just before noon, getting ready to depart for my swimming hole in the Red Spruce Brook, when a gust of wind blew the door shut; as I reopened the door and stepped outside a moment in the process, I happened to notice a swarm of large flying insects just emerging from the woods to the south-southeast. Moving slowly upslope toward the northwest, an enormous swarm of wild honey bees had soon engulfed half of my entire outcrop, forming a veritable cloud perhaps a hundred feet in diameter, its bulk concentrated five to twenty feet above the ground.

The center of the swarm passed a little to the southwest (though its outer fringe brushed the walls of my cabin), and the bees then gradually exited through a sort of alleyway in the vegetation, just above the west or northwest corner of the outcrop. Not twenty yards above this corner, they surrounded their queen in a tight, triangular cluster about sixteen inches on a side, suspended from the arching crown of a smallish pine tree. They were still there the next morning when I closed up the cabin and departed for the valley; undoubtedly, the bees moved on soon afterward, searching for shelter and a new home in the hollow of a tree.

On the night preceding the porcupine's visit described in an earlier chapter, I witnessed a partial lunar eclipse from my cabin. The spectacle was noteworthy because a slight haze in the sky rendered the darkened portion completely invisible and the arc of the Earth's shadow distinct. But what was truly extraordinary from my perspective derived from my lack of foreknowledge of the event and from the fact that I chanced to view it from its very earliest manifestation: The almost imperceptible nibbling away of the left corner of the full moon's face seemed inexplicable, until the phenomenon had advanced to the point where its identity suddenly became obvious to me. Up to then, I had observed this eclipse as an innocent in a "state of nature," as a prehistoric man might have done.

On February 11, 1987, I entered this description in my journal:

> *Late in the afternoon I happened to be gazing at the nearly-full moon, just risen near Lake Awosting, when a very distant jet airplane with a visible vapor trail about one to two degrees in length crossed over the moon, bisecting it, as the aircraft passed from right to left on a slight incline. The plane and its trail were not visible on the lunar disk. But with a white trail on either side after the plane emerged, the moon momentarily took on the appearance of the ringed planet Saturn!*

There is a natural phenomenon that I observe frequently, but with poor definition, from my cabin; I have observed it with greater clarity from other points on the mountain. It may be seen only when the observer is facing toward the precise anti-solar position—that is to say, directly opposite to the sun. The observation may best be made by looking in very clear weather at a uniformly tree-covered surface at least a thousand yards or so in distance and at a lower elevation than the observer, with the sun about to set, or just risen, to one's rear.

A convenient place for viewing this phenomenon is the cliff top of the "Near Trapps," easily accessible from Route

44/55 where it passes through a notch in the Shawangunk escarpment. But my earliest clear observation of it occurred while camping in 1988 not far from the Five-Mile Post, on the high overlook above Ann's Spring. I was looking east-southeastward just as the mid-August sun was getting ready to set behind me. The forested mountain slopes were bathed in low-angled sunlight. Suddenly my eyes came across a small area of enhanced reflectivity somewhere below Castle Point, just above the line of shadow that was inching up the mountain slopes as the sun descended to my rear. The spot seemed flat and featureless, almost hazy, yet appeared brighter than the surrounding foliage. Ten minutes later, on the verge of sunset, I noticed this spot had crept slightly upward and to the right. It was then I identified this as the same phenomenon I had seen and puzzled about a number of times as an airplane passenger. Finally, at home in the Shawangunks, I had come to understand its nature:

Looking at a forest canopy from this distance and under these conditions, one ordinarily sees sharply defined shadows interspersed with the brightly sunlit, foliage-covered branches. But at a point 180 degrees from the sun, there is a total absence of visible shadow. No matter how irregular the surface or peculiarly angled the tree branches, every shadow in that immediate vicinity will be cast directly away from the observer, blocked from view by the sunlit surface to which it owes its origin. The absence of visible shadow explains both the greater reflectivity per unit of surface area and the flat, featureless "haziness" of the spot.

I dubbed this optical curiosity *anti-solar enhancement of apparent arboreal albedo*. Later I learned this is one of several related visual effects known to scientists as *heiligenschein*. If it lacks the drama of some celestial or atmospheric events, it is nevertheless unique in being so wholly terrestrial a phenomenon. Looking into a distant forest at this warm, bright spot is much like making friendly eye contact with an individual among a sea of faces, as if the forest is exchanging greetings with the observer to herald the start or close of a summer's day. But like the sound made by the proverbial tree that falls in the forest, this phenomenon depends for its very existence on the sensory perception of an animate being.

By the Same Author

The Early History of Kingston & Ulster County, N.Y.

Tales from the Shawangunk Mountains:
A Naturalist's Musings, A Bushwhacker's Guide

The Huckleberry Pickers: A Raucous History of the Shawangunk Mountains